Choosing the Right Camp

1995–96 Edition

Choosing the Right Camp

1995-96 Edition

The Complete Guide to the Best Summer Camp for Your Child

Richard C. Kennedy and
Michael Kimball

TIMES **T** BOOKS

RANDOM HOUSE

Copyright © 1992, 1994 by Richard C. Kennedy and Michael Kimball
All rights reserved under International and Pan-American Copyright Conventions.
Published in the United States by Times Books, a division of Random House, Inc., New York and
simultaneously in Canada by Random House of Canada Limited, Toronto.

This work was originally published in different form in 1992 by Times Books,
a division of Random House, Inc.

Library of Congress Cataloging-in-Publication Data
Kennedy, Richard C.
Choosing the right camp, 1995–96 edition : the complete guide
to the best summer camp for your child / Richard C. Kennedy and
Michael Kimball. — 1st ed.
p.   cm.
ISBN 0-8129-2490-8
1. Camps—United States—Directories. 2. Outdoor recreation for
children—United States—Directories. I. Kimball, Michael.
II. Title.
GV193.K46   1992
796.54′2′02573—dc20   92-4573

Book design by Claire Naylon Vaccaro

Manufactured in the United States of America on acid-free paper
1   3   5   7   9   10   8   6   4   2
Second Edition

My thoughts and feelings about camps in general, and Camp Kieve (and other camps like it) in particular, have been forming over a lifetime. My mother and father started me on a lifetime of optimistic quest because they chose to invest themselves wholly in founding a small, focused educational institution in the bedrock belief that people are perfectible and that each of us makes a difference. My wife and I have tried to live our lives according to that tenet, and we are proud that our son and daughter-in-law are carrying on this work.

—Richard C. Kennedy

With love and pride to my children, Jesse and Sarah (who, for a short time in their adolescence, were beneficiaries of the Kennedy magic), and to my wife, Glenna, who continues to teach us all about love, strength, and perseverance.

—Michael Kimball

Foreword

Traveling across the country, visiting dedicated educators who run camps that change young people's lives, has been an inspiration to me. At first, when I got out of my own backyard, I was surprised to find so many people like me, who believe that camps provide an ideal setting to get "under the skin" of young people. Having witnessed an exciting recurring theme in so many different places, I now realize that camps are an essential part of the educational culture of North America.

The lessons that youngsters learn at camp will serve them well throughout their lives. In fact, unless these lessons are learned somewhere (and camps may well provide the best classroom), all the physics and sophisticated economic theory learned later on will be useless. The foundation for a happy, productive life is and always will be a strong character, and what camps do best is help young people learn how to make challenging personal decisions, the aggregate of which is character.

Camps build their educational systems on a foundation of respect for the individual and a carefully contrived group of personal experiences for each camper. Counselors are chosen for their qualities as good role models; and then, within the framework of the camp program, campers and counselors learn together in a spirit of fun and cooperation. The most important lessons for campers are reinforced by the daily camp routine: learning to work hard to complete a task in a complex woodworking project; learning to share responsibility at cabin cleanup in preparation for inspection; learning how to work within a group toward a common goal when they are paddling into a headwind toward the next campsite. These are the lessons that a young man or woman will never forget!

At the end of a successful camp season, it should be easy for parents and campers alike to evaluate the experience. Does the camper feel better about himself? Is she kinder to others? Is he more tolerant? Fairer? More helpful? If this book helps people find the one invaluable right camping experience for their child, then it is an important book.

One final word about the selection process: When all is said and done, the question to ask about the camp you're considering is "Will my child get more than a recreational experience from this camp; will she also learn lessons that will guide her throughout her life?" If the answer is yes, you are probably choosing wisely.

—Richard C. Kennedy

Contents

Choosing the Right Camp

1995–96 Edition

Why This Book?

For many children, going away to camp is the first time (and the longest time) they will be away from home. It's their introduction into a social structure that is not home, not family, and not school. They are going out into an unfamiliar world, entrusted to unfamiliar adults. For the parents, it's often the first time they've let loose of their child.

In the United States, there are roughly four thousand residential (sleep-away) camps, and many more day camps, specialty camps, and agency camps. Most are good, but some aren't. A few are exceptional. With this vast number of camps to choose from, your chances of making a poor choice are great.

Unfortunately, most campers end up at a particular camp for the wrong reasons: because cousin Bart goes to that camp; because the school sends home a pamphlet; because the church gets a group discount; because Uncle Harry went there as a boy. Too many well-meaning but distracted parents fall into the first trap of choosing a camp: *They leave the decision to someone else.*

Choosing a camp should be something the potential camper and parents actively and energetically do together. Parents should be carefully fitting the camp to their child. You are planning an important and sometimes expensive adventure for your child. If you do a haphazard job, this potentially wonderful experience runs the risk of turning into an unhappy and possibly traumatic separation.

Going away to camp should be fun, instructive, and constructive. And so should the process of selecting a camp. The choice is, however, a critical one. This book will give you and your child the tools to rationally and happily sift through some of the best camps in the country. It is designed so that everybody in your family can take part in the process and have a good time doing it.

A Little
Camp History

Camps, like Broadway musicals, are exclusively part of the American experience. Nowhere else in the world is there anything quite like the American camp. But just as the musical grew out of European opera, so do our camps owe a debt to Europe for their beginnings.

In the late nineteenth century, a handful of camps was founded in the northeast United States, loosely patterned after the semi-militaristic youth movements in Victorian Britain and Germany. But the American camps quickly adapted to the American way of thinking. They dropped most of the militaristic practices from their doctrine and substituted a reverence for natural beauty and a belief in enhancing the physical and moral strength of the individual. Underlying this Americanized philosophy was the doctrine of noblesse oblige, which stated that the person fortunate enough to have been affected by the camp's strengthening process had an obligation to use those strengths in the service of others less fortunate.

This philosophy, which may sound paternalistic now, was tremendously appealing to the upper classes in nineteenth-century America. Each year the rosters of the founding camps would read like the social register. If you were born into this small but powerful segment of society in Boston or New York or Philadelphia, your camp was the first step in a logical educational progression that extended to an elite boarding school and, finally, to an Ivy League college.

Depending on your point of view, you might conclude that camps got off to a bad start, that they were run by and for a small, privileged segment of society. But it's precisely because they started out with a narrow but clear focus in the 1880s and 1890s that so many camps today play such an important role in the fabric of America. Furthermore, the early institutional integrity of many of the country's finest camps has stood the test of time over the past century, while countless camps born of passing educational fashion have long since been forgotten.

The Good Old Way

Those who founded the early camps may have unconsciously taken as their model Teddy Roosevelt, and it is easy to see why. The leader of the Rough Riders was a national hero. Born of privilege, he felt an obligation to lead. In order to do so, he had to prepare both his mind and his body in rugged, demanding environments. He had to learn how to compete; to play hard and to win fairly. Though born with weak eyes and chronic asthma, by sheer force of character this man was able to overcome his physical handicaps and organize a group of horsemen into a hardy and disciplined team.

Any boy attending one of the exclusive camps at the turn of the century (few girls went away to camp then) would have emulated Teddy Roosevelt, who would soon become president. He would have striven to be chosen best camper and thus earn the ornate silver bowl for his trophy case. Hopefully the first of many trophies, it would have laid the groundwork for his future at his camp, where he would eventually have to overcome the challenges of the grueling, long camping trip, equipped with only the barest necessities.

A young man's camp experience would teach him that only the strongest and the best—the individuals who won the most trophies—would earn the ultimate reward of being looked to for leadership. He would learn that a highly developed character, marked by honesty, courage, loyalty, perseverance, and a sense of justice, was the most important quality in life; and that a man without character is like a carriage without a horse—it won't go anywhere.

The Second Wave

World War I had a critical effect on camping, just as it did on all of America's cultural institutions. The unprecedented carnage of the war was followed in this country by a movement espousing the belief that the best way to eliminate the chance of future disasters like the Great War was to engage actively in the solution of society's ills. Those who founded America's second wave of camps during this postwar period were an important part of that movement.

Whether they knew it or not, the camp directors of the 1920s followed Woodrow Wilson's lead with the same fervor as their predecessors had taken the Roosevelt course. And although there were indeed differences between these two generations of camp founders, their similarities were far more profound. Both schools were idealist; both believed in personal sacrifice for the common good; both believed that education and training were essential ingredients if one were to achieve; and both were progressive, believing that a few good ideas put forth by a few good people could make a difference in the world.

And so it was that the neo-Victorian camps, just like their Victorian predecessors, continued in the tradition of institutional self-confidence and the notion that if you educate the elite properly, they will lead the rest of society out of the immoral excesses of the Gay Nineties and Roaring Twenties.

The Wilsonian era was a logical extension of the Teddy Roosevelt era. World War I spawned renewed vigor in the camping movement with the founding of many new camps whose goals and structure were similar to those of their predecessors. This is where girls' camps, similar in every way to boys' camps, got their start. Also born at this time were the first so-called agency camps, sponsored by YMCA and YWCA groups, churches, and scouting groups.

Hard Times

By the end of the 1920s, the camping industry was poised for a dramatic explosion in numbers. Existing camps had become mature institutions with fine reputations and full enrollments. The almost slavish desire of the newly rich to imitate older-money society gave promise of camping's first big expansion.

Then the stock market crash and Great Depression hit, putting an immediate and chilling halt to that promise. The resulting decade had its effects on camps just as it did on the rest of society.

The 1930s, therefore, became a time for the camps to fine-tune their existing programs, to consolidate their efforts, and to try to hold on to their clients. Enrollments suffered, and programs and facilities (which had never been elaborate anyway) were trimmed to barely fulfill the camps' missions. It became almost virtuous for a camp to have a poorly paid staff, most of whom were alumni and were thoroughly instilled with the values of the camp.

The average camp counselor was a college student who could afford to spend the summer in the healthy and productive (if low-paying) occupation of helping young people grow up. In effect, then, the 1930s saw little substantial change in American camps. Both the campers and the counselors continued to come from the same stratum of society. As the decade progressed, those camps that had weathered the storm of the Great Depression began to see bright prospects for the future.

The War Years

The advent of World War II in Europe in 1939 and America's entry into the war in 1941 gave a big boost to the American economy, in particular to American camps. From 1939 to 1941, camp enrollments climbed rapidly. In 1942 they skyrocketed. For the first time in many American households, mothers were taking jobs out of the house while their husbands were either in the service overseas or themselves working long hours in support of the war effort. Suddenly in many families there was nobody at home to take care of the children after school. And during those long summer vacations from school, a large number of Americans began looking to camps to serve as surrogate parents.

The well-established, traditional camps willingly answered this need, and their enrollments during the war years swelled. Because the war infused the economy with spendable income for a burgeoning American middle class, many people could for the first time afford to send their children to camp. The children would learn time-honored skills and get a taste of well-regulated but rugged independence, far from the boredom of their unsupervised homes and safe from the potential dangers of war should the enemy bomb the factories in the cities.

The well-established camps, with their high tuitions and old traditions, were not the only camps to prosper during the war. During this time many charitable agencies responded to the needs of disadvantaged city children by purchasing property in the country and founding new camps. This period saw a tremendous expansion of scouting camps, YMCA and YWCA camps, and church-affiliated camps.

These new agency residential camps and day camps had several things in common. First of all, they cost less than the traditional camps, even though their programs were patterned after the latters'. The new camps relied largely on volunteer help, and their facilities were often either rented or donated. In order to serve as many of their needy clients as possible, the new camps offered stays of much shorter duration than did the traditional camps. Nevertheless, a valuable service was being offered to a whole new group of Americans for the first time. Camping in America had become a more inclusive, democratic institution and would never again be reserved for only the wealthy.

The war affected the day-to-day operation of all camps just as it affected all other American institutions. Gasoline was hard to come by, as were sugar and meat. Management of camps was also complicated by the difficulty of staffing. Most young men and women were either in the service or directly involved in the war effort in some other way, so camps had to rely on a mix of fifteen- and sixteen-year-olds and men and women over forty.

In spite of these difficulties, it was a great adventure to go to camp in the early 1940s. Parents became accustomed to sending ration stamps along with tuition payments. Campers grew vegetables in victory gardens, and at dinner directors read letters from recent alumni serving overseas. The war was a reality, but parents felt that their children were safe and healthy out in the country, and the campers were learning important American traditions.

The Postwar Boom

The 1940s saw a second explosion in camping at the war's conclusion. Camping had already begun to serve children from all strata of society; now that the fighting was over, society unleashed a tremendous pent-up desire to turn its back on the tensions and privations of wartime and to construct a happy and productive peace-time future.

Optimism seemed almost limitless. America had emerged from the war as the most powerful nation the world had ever seen. We alone had the atomic bomb. We alone had the economic power to reconstruct Germany and Japan. And in our farms and factories we had the massive productive capacity to feed the world's hungry and provide the finished products and technology for the world's emerging nations. In short, the U.S. was leader of the world, and the sweeping postwar euphoria gave rise to a massive expansion in American business and industry. Among the beneficiaries was camping.

For nearly twenty years, a host of camps were founded on a shoestring by ambitious young men and women who hoped to cash in on not only the baby boom but the fact that now millions of working-class families could afford to send their children to camp.

This new American middle class—people who had grown up penniless through the Great Depression—was suddenly able to emigrate from the cities where they had been raised to smaller, cleaner, quieter communities, where they brought up their own families. Low interest rates, benefits from the GI Bill, and a generous economy all meant that they could afford not only mortgages on their own suburban homes but also a few extras, like new appliances, cars, and even two-week summer vacations. This middle-class affluence, along with the promise for an even more plentiful future, became the American Dream.

But the dream was often impossible to realize. Developers of many large-scale suburban developments produced communities that somehow missed the bucolic essence of the dream. Houses were densely packed together, each a replica of the unit on either side. Yards looked the same; furniture looked the same; automobiles looked the same. Families even began resembling one another, often consciously or unconsciously emulating the middle-class families portrayed on television shows like *The Donna Reed Show, Father Knows Best,* or *Leave It to Beaver.* One of the jokes about these neighborhoods was that when a man came home at night after work, he ran the risk of walking into a number of houses before he found his own wife and children.

Camps prospered during this time because they offered children the opportunity to leave the rigid conformity of the suburbs for at least part of the summer. Perhaps more important, parents were motivated by a highly competitive social order that awarded a certain status for sending a child to camp.

Given this kind of social climate, it is no wonder that many of the camps founded in the 1950s and early 1960s were very similar to one another. Many were built on some of the traditions established by their progenitors. However, because they were new and often undercapitalized, these camps simply could not afford the luxuries of the older camps—such as a low staff-to-camper ratio, a wide variety of activities, experienced management, or a geographically diverse clientele.

Instead, the founders (who were often physical education instructors in the new suburban high schools, looking for new ways to market their skills) ran the camps the way they knew best. They saw to it that they had one or more good playing fields and then went about trying to attract to their staff a few of the best local high school or college athletes, at low salaries.

Naturally, these new camps specialized in competitive athletics. Their tuition structure was geared to the local community, where campers, staff, and director alike all lived during the winter. Unfortunately, the camps' success or failure was almost completely dependent upon the wisdom, vitality, and commitment of the directors, many of whom lacked both business skills and a cohesive philosophy of education.

Modern Times: The 1970s and 1980s

Not surprisingly, the postwar camps had the highest incidence of failure in the 1970s. Often, the director decided to sell his camp property (at a great profit) to land developers. Sometimes the camps succumbed to competition, unable to attract campers or keep up their facilities. Or perhaps local tax rates and other operating costs forced them to close.

In addition to those problems, the postwar camps faced the emergence in the 1960s and early 1970s of a completely new camping phenomenon—the specialty camp. Responding to the needs of a particular group of people, specialty camps were the product of two characteristics of the 1960s: a celebration of individuality and a pragmatic view of education. To those factors was added the continuing (and almost religious) belief of urban and suburban Americans that truth, beauty, and peace could best be found in the woods, and America embarked on yet another full-blown camping trend.

If you were fat and wanted to be thin; if you wanted to know more about rocketry or salamanders, a particular language or culture, a sport or creative art, you could now find a specialty camp specifically designed just for you. The added opportunities were plain to see. Suddenly a great many youngsters who had never found success in athletics or the competitive activities of traditional camps were attracted to camping. The kinds of skills offered at the new specialty camps were easily measured and easily marketed. The camps were staffed by people with a compelling interest in the special endeavor and easily discernible credentials. Parents could now watch their child become a better mathematician in a week or attain a new level of virtuosity with the tuba.

At first, attracting campers to specialty camps was not a problem, precisely because the target group was so narrow and thus easily located. Bulletin boards in high school computer rooms all over the country were covered with broadsides describing the best computer camps. Language departments, performing arts departments, and physical education departments were bombarded as well. The camp director simply used his network of acquaintances, in his particular specialty at colleges and universities, to find counselors who were proficient in particular skills and who were anxious to pass along their proficiency in a pleasant summertime environment.

The founding director of these camps was often a person in his mid-thirties, both devoted to his specialty and anxious to cash in on his experience and augment his teaching salary. Many of these budding entrepreneurs dreamed of eventually running the camp full-time and getting out of the academic rat race forever.

Unfortunately, like the directors of sports camps, few of these directors were experienced in business. In their zeal to offer the best, they often overspent on facilities or specialized equipment or both. Whether they leased their facilities or owned them outright, many of these directors simply borrowed more money than was prudent in the beginning phase of a business.

And, like the sports-camp directors, since their educational experience had been specialized, they had little appreciation for the relatively short attention span of youngsters or their need to be exposed to a wide variety of experiences. The campers' biggest complaint was, "It's boring; there's nothing to do in our free time." As a result, many of these camps suffered from having a program that was so narrow that it would not attract campers to return year after year.

Adding to these problems was the recession of the early 1980s and the resultant cut-throat competition among the glut of specialty camps, not to mention a renewed "back to the basics" approach to education. Many specialty camps did not survive the decade.

Today and Tomorrow

As we enter the second century of American camping, we once again find ourselves in a period of consolidation for camping in America. The inflation in real estate prices has discouraged people from starting camps because the price of property would make the investment imprudent.

However, the market for campers is stronger than ever before. There are many more single-parent families and families in which both parents are employed. Increasing numbers of these families are becoming aware that they sometimes need help in fulfilling their parenting roles. They see camp as a way to answer some of their children's needs and to add new dimensions to their children's lives. To them, camps offer opportunities that are beyond the time or resources of either the family or the children's schools—opportunities that will last a lifetime.

What to Look For in the Best Camps

First, a Little Learning Theory

Although camp should be an enjoyable experience, with plenty of recreation, the chief mission of the finest camps has always been educational—and it remains so today. Every camper ought to expect to learn lessons of lasting value at his or her camp. My theory of learning (which is also, not coincidentally, espoused by the best camps) is best explained by the acronym ASK:

> Attitude
> Skills
> Knowledge

Knowledge

I think the most overrated of all the components that make up learning is *knowledge,* whether it is knowledge of English grammar, mathematics, history, or physics. In fact, most schools used to equate learning with knowledge alone. They believed that the more theoretical knowledge they could cram into their students' heads, the more learning had taken place (and some schools still believe this!). Even today, the quality of some colleges and universities is measured by the number of books in their libraries or the scholarly attainment of their faculty. However, of all the learning that goes on in the best camps, knowledge is the least important ingredient. Knowing the genus and species of a clam, for example, does not help a camper revere nature.

Camp is an experience of short duration—at most, eight weeks. That is simply not enough time to acquire a great deal of knowledge. Even in specialty camps that concentrate on academics, a camper's short stay is fractured. She must divide her time between so many pursuits that she is simply unable to employ the concentration necessary for gaining lots of knowledge. Wise camp directors realize these limitations (and the limitations of their staffs) and leave most of the knowledge part of the learning equation to the schools.

Skills

A more vital part of learning is the acquisition of a wide variety of *skills*. Campers at the best camps learn everything from how to make friends to tying knots, from staying clean to hitting a backhand shot in tennis. Because these skills require the kind of learning that sometimes creates friction between a parent and child, they are best learned in an unhurried, unthreatening environment—away from home.

Who of us as a child hasn't been furious at a parent who constantly nagged about how messy our room was? And who of us as a parent hasn't been furious at the child for deliberately living in a pigpen of a room? At the best camps, acquiring neatness skills is not a problem because each cabin group is expected to cooperate in keeping the cabin tidy, and the groups receive communal rewards depending upon how well they measure up in the daily inspection. At the best camps, the routines of daily life are deliberately established to teach campers the skills of family living.

Attitude

By far the most important ingredient of the learning system employed by the best camps is *attitude*. A well-run camp is able to evaluate quickly and accurately the character of each camper and is then able to formulate an explicit or implicit plan to address both his strengths and weaknesses.

Camp is an ideal place to learn how to be considerate of other people, how to be a good sport, how to appreciate your good fortune, how to sustain a high degree of effort in order to achieve a worthy goal. In the best camps, staff members are carefully chosen not only for their expertise in a particular field but, more important, for their abilities as mentors—role models.

🦎

The best camps, then, employ a learning system that might at first seem to be upside down, or at least contrary to the traditional views of what is most important and what is least important about learning. This applies even to specialty camps. In a specialty sailing camp, for example, *knowledge* about nomenclature and tactics is important—but not as important as the sailing *skills* learned both in class and in regattas. But together they are not as important as the *attitude*—toward sailing in particular and life in general—that the young campers take from their camping experience.

The best camps are designed and run by optimists. The guiding philosophy of all of these institutions is that people, particularly young people, are perfectible. By providing a succession of personalized and individualized experiences, these camps, year after year, have a lasting effect on the attitude of the campers entrusted to them.

When you are evaluating camps, make sure that the one you choose has as its principal goal the enrichment of its campers by bringing about measurable changes in their attitudes, and that the camp has a good track record of success in achieving that goal. If you employ any less demanding criterion, you are cheating yourself and your child.

On to Specifics: What to Look (and Watch Out) For

Location (Distance; Physical Surroundings)

Consider the importance of fresh water, salt water, a mountain environment, etc. At first, both the camper and the parent might be tempted to want the camp close to home. But the purpose of going away to camp is to begin loosening the ties of dependence, so some distance from home is appropriate. Almost all good camps are in scenic spots, and some locales are spectacular. If your child wants to specialize in an activity (riding, sailing, mountain climbing), make sure the camp is in an appropriate place for that activity. Maybe most important, how does the place *feel* to you? For however long the camper plans to stay, this will be his or her home away from home.

Size

Does the camper feel more comfortable in smaller or larger groups? Does she like the personality of a small institution or the possibilities of a big one? If it is a big camp, is it designed so that campers live and act in small, autonomous groups? If it is a small camp, is there enough diversity of peers and activities? What is the ratio of campers to staff, and is it appropriate for the camp's educational mission?

Gender

Since your child probably goes to a school with children of the opposite sex, he is probably already at ease with them, to some degree anyway. Camp is different from school because it is less formal, socially more intense, a place for experimenting with new activities and taking risks. Some feel that it is natural to be with both sexes; others feel that single-sex camps eliminate the boy-girl tensions often present among older campers.

Age

There should be enough campers your child's age so that the program will be appropriate for her and so that she will be able to make close friendships.

Geographical Representation

Beware of sending your child to a camp populated only by people who live where you do in the winter. When that is the case, the social order established in the winter is simply replicated at summer camp. Going away and meeting new people presents campers with an opportunity to break out of the molds they may feel trapped in.

On the other hand, your camper will probably want the security of knowing that some others from his area are part of the camp community. In the final analysis, too much diversity is just as unhealthy as too little diversity. Your choice will (and should) depend on your child's level of self-confidence.

If there is a significant international population, are the international campers an integral part of the camp community, or might they feel left out? How do the American campers feel about the international campers?

Duration of Stay

A good question to ask is simply "How many campers attend this camp for the length of time we want?"

Many camps will tell you that a camper needs seven weeks to benefit from the experience they offer. But since we feel that the most valuable time a child can spend is unhurried time with his or her family, we advocate a four-week camp program.

Why four weeks? A camper should be away from home for enough time to progress through the natural development stages: from homesickness to uncertainty to confidence and pride. Any time period shorter than two weeks allows her simply to count the days until the experience is over. More than four weeks, and he may find that the day-to-day routine becomes boring.

In any case, it is important that your camp not try to cram into four weeks a program designed for eight weeks. If there are split sessions (say, two 3-week sessions), there should be a different and appropriate program for both the short- and long-term campers.

If many campers stay the whole season, it may be a tip-off that this is a place where parents send their kids to get them out of their hair; if so, there may be some unhappy campers there. And in the presence of mostly whole-season campers, short-term campers might feel like outsiders.

Cost

Two things are true when it comes to paying for your camp. A good camp experience is a vital educational experience. And you generally get what you pay for. In other words the best camps, while not necessarily the most costly, aren't going to be cheap, either.

First, make sure that you are comfortable with the camp's fee. If you can't afford it, don't kid yourself. Most of the campers' families will be financially like yours. However, be sure to find out if financial aid (in the form of scholarships) is available, and if so, who qualifies. (Incidentally, camp is one of those nice things that some grandparents like to do for their grandchildren.)

In making your plans, be sure to factor in *all* costs: Besides tuition, that includes transportation, extra fees, equipment, snacks, etc. Be careful of camps that charge an extra fee for some of their programs. If you couldn't afford these extras, you wouldn't want your son or daughter feeling left out when his or her friends are participating. Avoid a camp if you can't afford its extras.

Structure of the Camp

A camp's structure—how it is organized and maintained—will tell you a lot about its educational philosophy. (Parents, rather than campers, are probably better able to make this judgment.) A camp's structure should provide a lively educational institution, one that has integrity and also adapts to changing conditions. When, how, and by whom the camp was founded could also tell you a lot about its philosophy.

The stability of a camp is a good indication of its structure and philosophy. Look at the camp's past performance and its prospects for the future. A good clue to a camp's stability is whether or not it has been under sustained leadership.

The structure should be one that ensures that the camp will continue even if the current director leaves. Be wary of camps that are completely dependent upon the efforts of one person or one family.

If the owner and the manager are different, it is important to determine what their relationship is, who is making policy, and whether the owner and manager agree on policy and goals. If not, a new manager may come on board with different ideas for running the camp. You may want to ask camp directors what their future plans are when the current owner sells or dies.

Staff

All conscientious parents are concerned about the people to whom they entrust their children. The camp should be able to provide you with information about the camp staff that will assure you that they are careful in the hiring and screening of their workers.

Among other things, questions about educational background and experience of the staff will give you an indication of whether the camp exists for the benefit of the children or whether it's primarily a business designed to make maximum profits. If the latter is the case, parents should pay particular attention to the manner in which staff is hired and supervised.

Often the staff reflects the interests and values of the director, so you should get to know the director before entrusting your child to his camp. If there is much turnover in the senior or junior staff, it may be a good indication of an unhappy environment.

Some questions you should ask are:

Where does the staff come from?

How old are they? How experienced?

What kind of training do they have?

What criteria does the director use in hiring?

Are there safeguards in place to prevent sexual or physical abuse? (For example, do staff people always work in pairs when they are with campers?)

In case there were sexual or physical abuse, how would the director handle the situation?

Goals and Values

What does the camp aim to accomplish for its campers? Does it have a serious, well-thought-out curriculum designed to meet certain goals, or is it primarily recreational?

The goals and values of a camp should be expressed *clearly* by the camp catalog and by any of its staff people at any given time.

Regardless of its intent, the most important question you can ask about any camp is "Does the camp live up to its goals?" Or does it only superficially adhere to the stated goals?

Program

The activities offered by the camp and the qualifications of those teaching them (as well as their educational purpose) all give a good indication as to the quality and intentions of the camp.

Most activities should be attempting to (a) change attitudes; (b) teach skills; and/or (c) impart knowledge. In order to accomplish this, there should be a high level of teaching ability in these activities.

Does the program match the stated goals? A camp that states that its goal is to build self-esteem and then offers "single-winner" games like red rover or musical chairs isn't matching its program to its goals.

The balance between required and optional activities also reveals a lot about the camp's attitude toward its campers as well as its philosophy. For example, is there a lot of letter-writing time or rest time in the schedule? Are there a lot of pick-up games? Some camps have a well-written statement of educational philosophy, but in practice the program is lax and designed only for fun.

There should be an easily discernible educational component to the program that is appropriate to the age and ability of the campers. And although stability is a necessary feature of the best camps, the program needs to change occasionally to reflect changes in the times.

Facilities

Camp facilities should be adequate for their use, up-to-date, and in good repair, and the camp should be making adequate investments in its plant and equipment. The appearance of a campus can tell a great deal about a camp's attitude. Grounds should be well maintained and attractive; buildings—even if rustic—should be in good repair. Finally, check to see if there are any facilities that the camp should have which are either inadequate or nonexistent.

Health and Safety

The questions to ask are: What happens if there is an accident on a trip? There is an accident on the waterfront? A camper was to show signs of depression?

The staff should be well trained in health and safety issues. A good camp will have an infirmary and at least one nurse on the premises, as well as a working relationship with a nearby hospital and a doctor on call at all times.

There should be clear protocols and policies in place. For example, at what point in the protocol of accident, injury, or sickness does the camp contact the parent? These are all questions that you should ask the director if answers are not provided in their catalog.

Feeding

In matters of feeding, camps should not be vague. Either they have a clearly defined policy or they don't. What are the credentials of the person planning the menu? The person responsible for preparing the food? What food is on a week's menu? What food is typically sent out on a short trip? Long trip? Is the food nutritious? Are arrangements made for special diets—for example, for campers who are diabetic, vegetarian, overweight, or allergic? *Do campers like the food?*

Intuition

Very important: Trust your feelings, and trust the feelings of other clients. Do the style, tone, and atmosphere of the camp feel right for you? Is there a recurring theme from the camp's publications, leadership, and clientele that appeals to you? Can you imagine your child fitting into this camp comfortably?

Specialty Camps, Day Camps, and Agency Camps

For this book we have chosen mostly residential camps with general programs rather than day camps (camps that do not provide overnight accommodations), agency camps (camps sponsored by churches or agencies such as YMCA, Girl Scouts, Boys Clubs, etc.) or specialty camps (rocket camps, computer camps, etc.).

In our experience, residential camps with general programs provide a greater variety of opportunities as well as the sort of institutional longevity and financial stability not found as much in specialty camps, agency camps, and day camps. And because agency camps and day camps usually serve only the children from their surrounding communities, those camps would be inappropriate candidates for this book, which seeks to serve a much wider audience.

However, any of these types of camps might be the right choice for your family. For children who are absorbed in a singular activity—horseback riding, for instance—an equestrian specialty camp might be the best choice. Perhaps a family's budget does not allow for the expense of a residential camp. In that case, a nearby day camp or agency camp might provide a wonderful experience for your child.

Choosing a Specialty Camp

Some people might think that choosing a good specialty camp for their child is easier than choosing a good general camp. After all, there are fewer to choose from, and you already know precisely which special activity you're looking for. The first thing parents should know is that just because a camp features a specialized field in its title—Annie Oakley Horsemanship Camp for Girls—doesn't mean that its equestrian program is any better, or even as good, as that offered by a good general camp that has concentrated on horsemanship for decades. When looking for a specialty camp for your child, always look beyond the camp name and delve into the substance of the camp's program.

That's not to say that single-specialty camps, by definition, are shallow. This book lists a number of specialty camps that have both a solid concentration on a specialized area and a sound educational and structural foundation: Interlochen (performing arts), Windridge and Tamarack (tennis), Cape Cod Sea Camps and Camps Seagull and Seafarer (sailing), and the Clara Barton/Elliott Joslin Camps for Children with Diabetes, to name a few.

Specialty camps, like general camps, run the gamut from day camps that may run for one day to several weeks, to residential camps that may run the entire summer. When looking for camps that cater to a specific field of interest, one place to start might be in your library. *Peterson's Summer Opportunities for Kids and Teenagers* lists hundreds of camps nationwide according to program offerings. The *American Camping Association Guide to Accredited Camps* is another source, although it lists only those camps that have applied for ACA accreditation (and many fine camps do not).

From your long list, you can make phone calls and send for brochures to get a sense of whether the field of interest is one in which a particular camp excels or if it's simply one of many activities. Another source of specialty camps is the advertising pages of magazines devoted to that particular interest. Many specialty camps send promotional materials to schools. Posters advertising basketball camps, for instance, might be displayed around the school gym. National organizations are another good resources for specialty camps; often they sponsor camps themselves.

If you and your child feel that a specialty camp is best, you should choose a camp with the same care and attention as you'd choose any good camp.

Diversity

The potential problem with specialty camps (the chief reason many have been short-lived) is that there isn't enough to do. In other words, after spending three hours on the ice at hockey camp, does the camp provide a carefully structured program of varied educational and recreational activities, or are the kids left on their own with a couple of Frisbees and a playing field? On the other hand, is the camper practicing ice hockey for twelve hours a day? Even the most ardent young devotee of any interest is bound to feel restless if not provided with some variety of alternative activities (consider math camp, computer camp).

At the best specialty camps, the specialty is a rich, main course in a wonderful smorgasbord of activities. At Interlochen, for example, after spending two hours playing in a wind ensemble, a young oboist will charge down to the waterfront with his friends for an hour of sailing or diving instruction.

Age

Make sure the instruction is appropriate for *both* the age and skill level of your child. One way you can do this is by checking the schedule of instruction offered. Are there enough beginning, intermediate, or advanced levels to meet your child's needs, or does the camp generalize about levels?

Size

Check the number of campers against the size of the teaching staff. The instructor-to-camper ratio will tell a lot about whether your camper will be active and attended to or will spend a lot of time standing in lines or sitting around. Bear in mind that some specialties (baseball, for example) require slightly less individual attention than, say, rock climbing, so when comparing staff-to-camper ratios, make sure you're comparing apples with apples.

Facilities

Very important. Most specialties require specialized equipment and specific facilities. A good sailing camp obviously requires an extensive waterfront (or several waterfront sites) and enough sailboats in top condition so that every camper has his own craft for a good amount of time every day.

Many specialty camps (especially sports camps) use the facilities of a nearby college or school, yet they attempt to instruct a greater number of campers than would ordinarily be participating at any one time during the school year. In other words, the campus isn't adequate for the numbers. Incidentally, school campus camps are also prone to the first problem mentioned: not enough variety of activities to keep campers engaged.

Instructors

Instructors in specialty fields need to be special people indeed. Although they should be experts in the field themselves, particularly those teaching advanced levels, it's more important that they be gifted educators. They must be nurturing individuals who respect the individuality of the children in their care and who are devoted to the educational and philosophical mission of the camp as a whole. Unfortunately, some very talented people can also be impatient, insensitive, or even insulting with the young people whom they teach. Such a person can inadvertently do more harm than good by turning campers away from an activity they have grown to love.

Because some specialty camps you might be considering are located far from home, it may not be possible to meet all the instructors. As we've said before, be sure to speak with the director. Ask what he or she looks for in a staff member. Find out what the instructors do in the off-season and how long they've been associated with the camp. Be sure that the camp's overall philosophy coincides with your own. If the camp mission is solely to further skills, with no attention to ethical or character development, you'd do well to consider other camps.

Big Names

Beware of camps, particularly sports camps, that use names of celebrities in their titles or promotional materials. Just because a basketball star once made an appearance or has sold his name to an institution does not mean that he has anything to do with the instruction, planning, or administration of the camp. Even if he does, what do you know about the star's *teaching* philosophy until you investigate? Ask questions.

Structure

In our opinion, a good specialty camp should be structured in many ways like a good general camp. Be aware of how financially secure the camp is, how long it's been operating, and how committed the owners are to its endurance. Some camps are set up by a local coach or athlete trying to cash in on his notoriety or some available facilities, with no long-range goals for either the camp or campers.

Intuition

Intuition is very important. Be aware of how you *feel* about what people say and what they're doing at the camp. Be sure to ask yourself: *Do these people care about my son or daughter as an individual? Do they work only on developing skills, or do they have a higher purpose?* Finally, ask the director for a list of current and former campers, and then contact those families to see how they feel about the camp.

Choosing a Day Camp

By design, day camps are close to home, and that gives parents a huge advantage: You can visit the camp. Do, by all means. Seeing the camp in operation is our first and most important recommendation. Talk to the directors and counselors, and make sure that you feel comfortable with everything that is going on.

Duration

Day camps are almost always shorter in duration than residential camps. The obvious advantage of the shorter program (and lack of resident facilities) is that day camps are therefore affordable to most families. By the same token, the shorter program (and lack of resident facilities) makes it difficult to create a sustained sense of independence that is one of the most valuable features of a child's camp experience.

Geographic Representation

Another benefit of residential camps is that a child has the chance (and challenge) of making new friends, taking some social risks, and making a new place for himself in a new group. Children at day camps, however, usually come from the same area, often the same school. The disadvantage is that a child will find herself in a social structure very much like the one at school, with the same cliques and the same best (and worst) friends. Find out if the camp makes an effort to group children from different schools, different ages, or the opposite sex.

Staff

This is critical. Because day camps are apt to be less grounded than residential or specialty camps in a philosophical or educational mission, and because the operating budget is not as large, selection and training of counselors is often not as carefully done as at residential camps. Be sure to ask how the staff is chosen and supervised. Make sure that safeguards are in place so that, for example, an individual counselor will not work in an isolated setting with a single child.

Health and Safety

Day camps are often busy places, with lots of things going on at once. Because staff-to-camper ratios are usually smaller and counselors younger and less experienced (reflecting the smaller operating budget), and because there isn't the 24-hour community present at resident camps, it's more likely that a child might find herself unattended. Questions about health and safety procedures should be answered to your satisfaction before you send your child to any camp. You should know what training counselors are given and what emergency measures are in place should an injury or sickness occur.

Goal and Values

Most day camps exist to give local children the kinds of opportunities campers get at any camp. They teach swimming, sports, and other outdoor activities, along with some arts and crafts. As in all camps, an educational component should be part of the fun and games, and the entire staff should be attuned to that mission. Goals need not be grandiose; at a week-long day camp, far-reaching aspirations would be unrealistic and cause for suspicion. The camp's mission should be clear, and it should be achievable. Ask the director what the camp aims to do for its campers. If the answer is unclear, the camp may be nothing more than a big, unfocused playground.

Intuition

Again, because it is easy to visit a local day camp, you should visit all those in your area—and speak with the directors—before making your final decision. Then pay attention to how you feel. Do you like the way the children are treated? Do you like the way they treat each other? Do you like the director personally? Do you like the counselors? Consulting your feelings after you have learned all you can about a camp is the most important bit of research you can do.

Choosing an Agency Camp

Agency camps, like day camps, provide summer camp opportunities for many children who might not otherwise be able to attend camp. All agency camps have several things in common. First of all, the camp's mission will generally reflect that of its funding source, which means there's a good chance that the camp has goals for campers that are other than simply recreational. Because agency camps, like day camps, are often close to home, parents have a great opportunity to visit the camp in session and see exactly what's going on.

Cost

Agency camps are usually less expensive than other residential camps because they receive funding from their sponsoring agency, whether the Boy Scouts of America, a local YWCA or Girls Club, a 4-H chapter or church. That's a big advantage for many families. However, a limited budget often translates to shorter duration—and as we've said, it generally takes at least two to three weeks for a camp experience to engender in a young person a real sense of independence and pride of accomplishment. Also, because agency camps are usually accessible to more families, you will probably find a population of kids from roughly the same socioeconomic and geographic area, with the same social hierarchy from their local schools. See if the camp makes an effort to challenge kids to make new friends.

Structure

The camp's structure will depend on the solidity of its funding agency. Generally, well-established institutions such as the Boy Scouts and the Girl Scouts are financially sound and draw on many years of camping experience. However, you should pay attention to the stability of the camp itself. Any camp with frequently changing management is a place likely in disarray.

Staff

Staff-to-camper ratios at agency camps are probably smaller than at private camps, reflecting the smaller operating budget. Smaller ratios often translate to more athletics (where fewer counselors can facilitate larger groups) and less personalized instruction. In the case of a camp that runs lots of athletics, make sure that camp policy (and adequate adult supervision) dictates that all campers, not just the stars, get equal opportunities to participate.

As we've pointed out, ratios are important, but not nearly as important as the staff's attitude and training. Happily, you can expect to find a well-trained (but not necessarily high-paid) staff at most agency camps, reflecting the time-tested missions of the parent agency.

Program

Agency camps often offer fewer activities than better-funded independent camps and have a larger number of campers participating in each one. Where an agency camp might have three things going on at any one time, another camp, like Maine's Hidden Valley, might be running fifteen activities. Parents should look at the camp's daily schedule to make sure the activities offered interest their child. Some agency camps (look at Camp Dudley YMCA, in this book, for example) offer programs as rich and varied as any in the country. You'll need to find out for yourself. While many great agency camps exist, there are also some where an unassertive child might find himself frequently out of the action.

Goals

As in all camps, the important question to ask is: What does the camp aim to do for its campers? And does this camp meet its goals?

How to Use
This Book

In order to determine America's fifty finest camps, the authors have employed a five-step process to evaluate hundreds of camps nationwide. The process is a simple one and does not involve visiting every camp that might be of interest. In fact, if the process is followed conscientiously, any family should be able to make a sound camp choice that is the very best for both the camper and parents. Best of all, choosing a camp provides the entire family with a special opportunity to spend some valuable time together.

The Five Steps
1. Dream Camp
2. Making the Long List
3. Letters to Camps
4. Making the Short List
5. Making Contact

Step One: Dream Camp

Do you all know exactly what you're looking for in a camp? If not, maybe you should think about it. *If you could create the ideal camp, what would it be like?*

Where would the camp be? At the ocean? On a lake? In the mountains? And what would your child like to learn? Archery? Horseback riding? Tennis? What kind of friends would she like to make? Boys or girls from other countries? From other parts of the United States? Does he want a camp that offers a lot of team sports or one that encourages individual challenges? Does she want to go off on long camping expeditions into the mountains or fifty miles down a river, or might she be happier staying close to camp?

After looking over some of the camps in this book (so that you all know the sorts of things camps offer), parents and campers alike should each design the ideal camp—their dream camp. (You'll find a *Dream Camp Checklist* on pages 39–40 in this book to help you.) What skills would your camper love to learn? What kinds of activities would he like to be offered? How long would she want to stay? What kinds of other campers and counselors would he like to share his adventure with?

Then think a little deeper and more broadly: What kind of outlook on life would this camp have? How would she want to be challenged? How would he like to be enriched?

When each of you has finished designing your dream camp, get together and compare notes. Be sure to talk about how your dream camps differ and, more important, how they are alike. Remember, this is just a dream stage and needn't be too specific. Leave room for flexibility. After learning more about what the best camps have to offer, you all may find that reality is better than your dreams. After all, most of these camps have had fifty years or more in which to improve on their dreams.

Step Two: Making the Long List

The second part of the process is to come up with a *long list* of approximately ten camps that seem to fit your Dream Camp Checklist. At this point, the opinions and experiences of friends and other family members are valuable. Your long list ought to include as wide a variety of camps as you might be interested in. But it should certainly exclude camps that don't fit your family budget, transportation abilities, or schedule. And it's important to exclude those with features that don't fit the camper's interests. For example, if the camp schedules two hours a day for mandatory horseback riding and your child hates horses, she probably won't like the camp.

The *Long List Checklist* (pages 45–48) will help define your choices. Because the checklist is fairly complete, there will no doubt be many questions you won't know the answers to. But that's okay. You're still not ready to make your final decision.

Step Three: Letters to Camps

The third part of the process is to write a short letter to the director of each of the ten camps that made your long list. In the letters you will simply express your interest in the camp and ask for information. We have printed a sample letter (page 49) that you can use as a model.

After you receive the information and you've had a chance to look it over, you'll want to write back to the directors of the most interesting camps (sample letter—page 49) with specific questions that the brochures might not have answered. After reading the section "What to Look For in the Best Camps" you'll have a good idea of the kinds of questions to ask in order to arrive at the most complete picture possible of the camps that interest you. Here you can also address your camper's particular needs, likes, and dislikes. For example, does the camp accommodate a certain diet? Or is there somebody there with advanced training in a particular field?

Step Four: Making the Short List

The fourth step is where the family fun and excitement begins. Once you receive responses from your ten camps, everyone concerned should independently evaluate the catalogs and letters and finish filling in the long list checklist. (It is important that you end up with roughly the same information from each of the camps, so that you're able to make a fair comparison.) You should all prepare to offer your opinions of your findings at a family meeting. By now you each are probably leaning toward one or two of your favorite camps. The purpose of this meeting is to end up with a short list of two or three camps that everybody can agree are the very best.

It's most important that everybody feel comfortable with the decision and that the only camps on that list are those that are attractive to *both* the camper and the parents. (In general, the farther along in the process, the greater should be the weight of the camper's opinion. However, this decision, like all important family decisions, should reflect the family's style.) Consensus is important if the experience is to succeed. Neither the child nor the parents should feel, now or later, that they were coerced into a choice.

Step Five: Making Contact

The fifth and final step before making your final choice—and this is vital—is for the parents and the child to come into physical contact with the two or three camps on the short list.

Obviously, the most meaningful contact would be a visit while the camp is in session, but that isn't always possible. The next best contact would be a meeting with the director or senior staff person if he or she is going to be near your home. A phone conversation with the director (if you are unable to meet him or her personally) is also valuable. The least effective (but perhaps only practical) contact is to view carefully the camp's video presentation—if one exists.

In any case, your contact with the camps should include discussions with recent campers and their families. When you complete this fifth and final step of the choice process, you all should feel confident about your choice and eager for the new adventure to begin.

Dream Camp Checklist

1. **Location**
   How far from home would you like to go?
   same country_____ same state_____
   within 100 miles_____ same region_____
   anywhere is fine_____

2. **Physical surroundings**
   What kind of physical surroundings would you like?
   country_____ suburbs_____ city_____
   lakeside_____ oceanside_____ mountains_____
   desert_____ anywhere_____

3. **Size**
   small_____ medium_____ large_____
   any size_____

4. **Gender**
   all boys_____ all girls_____ both boys and girls_____

5. **Age**
   How old do you want the other campers to be?
   same age_____ two-year spread_____
   three-year spread_____ five-year spread_____
   any age fine_____

6. **Geographical representation**
   Would you like a camp that has geographical diversity, or would you rather have more people from your part of the world? Where should they come from?

   my town_____ my state_____ several states_____
   several regions_____ several countries_____

7. **Duration**
   How long do you want to be able to stay?
   about one week_____ about two weeks_____
   about four weeks_____ more than four weeks_____

8. **Cost**
   How much do we want to spend?_____
   How much are we able to spend?_____

9. **Goals and values**
   Do we want a camp that is:
   primarily recreational?_____
   carefully designed to meet certain goals?_____ (If so, which goals would be important?)

10. **Program**
    Do we want a camp with:
    lots of structured activities?_____ lots of free time?_____
    In order of importance, list the activities you would want:

11. **Other features**
    What other facilities and features do we want the camp to have?

Checklist Guide

Location

Distance

Can you afford the transportation costs? Can you be there on visiting day? Can you pick her up, or will the camp provide transportation to the airport or bus or train station? Is it far enough away from home that he doesn't think you're hovering, yet close enough that you feel comfortable?

Physical Surroundings

If your camper has specific interests, like boating, riding, mountain climbing, etc., does the locale provide the necessary natural environment? Do the physical surroundings make you feel safe and comfortable? Do they seem attractive?

Size

Are there so many campers that the camp seems impersonal and institutional? Will an unassertive child feel lost and ignored? Or is there a low enough staff-to-camper ratio to ensure that the campers are well supervised and attended to?

On the other hand, are there enough people for her to have many friends to choose from? Are there enough people to support a diversified program? Is the camp so small that he might feel unchallenged?

Gender

Do we want our child to go to camp with both boys and girls or only one gender? Is it a place where a girl's self-esteem is valued?

Age

Do we want our child to learn to coexist and cooperate with both older and younger campers? Can we trust that the camp deals responsibly with the types of power structures that can occur among children of varying ages? Are there enough campers in our child's age group so that the program will reflect his needs and so that he will have enough friends?

Geographical Representation

Is this a camp that promotes harmony between campers from varying geographical backgrounds? Or are they more comfortable with campers from a narrower base? Are campers primarily from only one town or county?

Duration

How long will she be comfortable being away from home? How long will you be comfortable having her away? Will the camper's stay be long enough for him to go through the natural early anxieties yet short enough so that the routine doesn't become boring?

If there are split sessions, is there a separate and appropriate program for both the short- and long-term campers?

Cost

Be sure to add up *all* costs: transportation, crafts fees, and other extra fees, as well as extra pocket money for snacks and souvenirs. Remember, many camps offer scholarships. Be sure to find out who gets them and how much is offered.

Structure of Camp

Does the camp's overall structure make you confident that the camp will endure, or is it completely dependent upon the efforts of one person or one family? Has it been under sustained leadership, with a fairly ongoing philosophy? Is the camp owned and managed by different people? If so, are their philosophies the same?

Staff

What do you know about the director(s), counselors, and staff? Are these the kind of people you want as surrogate parents for your child?

Goals and Values

Does the camp express a clear aim for what it wants to accomplish for its campers? Do these goals and values coincide with yours? Most important of all: *Does the camp do what it says it does?*

Program

Does the program match the stated goals? Is it educational or just for fun? Is the program well run? Are the activities well taught? Is the program appropriate to the age and ability of the campers? Which activities does this camp concentrate on? Is there a good balance between required and optional activities?

Facilities

Are the facilities adequate to running the program effectively, efficiently, and safely? Are the facilities up-to-date? Does the camp seem to make adequate investments in plant and equipment? Are there any facilities that the camp should have that are either inadequate or nonexistent?

Health and Safety

How does the camp care for the health and safety of its campers? Are staff adequately trained in health and safety issues? Is there an infirmary? A nurse? A doctor? A relationship with a nearby hospital? What is the role of the health care specialists, and what is the role of the general staff in health care issues?

Feeding

Is the food nutritious? Appetizing? Are the kitchen and dining facilities adequate? Who runs these facilities? Are there provisions made for those with special dietary needs? What do last year's kids and parents say about the food?

Intuition

Important. How does the camp *feel* to you? On paper, the camp may look wonderful. But if something doesn't feel quite right, you'd be wise to keep looking.

Long List Checklist

CAMP_____

1. **Location**
   Distance: How far from home is it?_____ miles

   Physical surroundings: country_____ suburbs_____

   city_____ lakeside_____ oceanside_____

   mountains_____ desert_____

2. **Size**
   How many campers?_____

   campers per staff person_____ per bunkhouse_____

3. **Gender**
   Is the camp: boys only_____ girls only_____ both_____

4. **Age**
   youngest_____ oldest_____

   approximate number in camper's age group_____

5. **Geographical representation**
   Approximately what percentage of campers come from:

   your town_____ your county_____ your state_____

   your region_____ several states_____

   foreign countries_____

6. **Duration**
   How long do most campers stay?

   one or two weeks_____ three or four weeks_____

   five or six weeks_____ seven or eight weeks, or longer_____

7. Cost

How much does tuition cost?_____

Extra cost, including special equipment, programs, uniforms, and transportation:_____

Are there scholarships available?_____

How much?_____ For whom?_____

TOTAL_____

8. Structure of camp

When was it founded?_____

Has it been under sustained leadership?_____

Who owns it?_____

Who manages it?_____

Is it likely to endure beyond its present ownership/management?_____

Who is likely to take over?_____

9. Staff

Director's educational background:_____

Relevant experience:_____

How long has he or she been associated with the camp?_____

What is the ratio of staff_____ to campers_____?

How many counselors?_____

How old are the counselors?_____

How many repeat counselors?_____

How are the counselors chosen?_____

Where do they come from?_____

What criteria does the director use in hiring?_____

10. Goals and values

What does the camp aim to accomplish for its campers?_____

Does it have a serious, carefully planned curriculum designed to meet certain goals?_____

Does it aim to teach values, or is it primarily recreational?_____

Are the goals age-appropriate?_____

11. Program

What activities are available?_____

Which activities don't they offer?_____

Which unexpected activities are offered?_____

Are there any required activities that are unappealing?_____

12. Facilities

What facilities does the camp have to offer?_____

Are they well maintained?_____

Are they adequate for the program?_____

Are the grounds well maintained and attractive?_____

13. Health and safety

How does the camp care for the health and safety of its campers?_____

At the waterfront?_____ On trips?_____ At other potentially dangerous locations around camp?_____

Who is the health care specialist?_____

His/her training?_____

Staff training?_____

Infirmary?_____

Is there a nearby hospital?_____

In case of emergency, when and how does camp notify parents?_____

14. Feeding

Is the food nutritious? Well prepared?_____

Are the kitchen and dining facilities adequate?_____

Who runs these facilities?_____

His/her training and experience?_____

Provisions for special diets?_____

15. Intuition

How does this camp feel to you?_____ Is everybody in the family looking forward to the experience?_____

Letters to Camps

You should be prepared to write two letters to each camp. The first is simply a request for all of the camp's pertinent information. It need be no longer than a paragraph:

Camp Beaver Tail
Edge of Nowhere, MN 01234

Dear Camp Director:

Our son/daughter is nine years old. We're seriously considering sending him/ her to your camp. Please send us all the information you can about your camp. Thank you.

Sincerely,
Mom and Dad

The second letter should address any specific questions which were not satisfactorily addressed in the camp's brochures:

Camp Beaver Tail
Edge of Nowhere, MN 01234

Dear Camp Director:

Thank you for sending your camp's brochures and other information. We are interested in sending Pat to your camp, but we need the answers to some specific questions before we can make our final decision. We'd appreciate your attention to this matter at your earliest convenience.

Sincerely,
Mom and Dad

By this time, you will have a good idea of what questions to ask. For example, if your camper is a vegetarian, ask if there are vegetarian substitutions at *all* meals. If he or she has a problem with heights, ask if there are alternative worthwhile activities on mountain-climbing day.

Above all, remember that you are consumers. The camp is offering a service. Getting the very best for your child is what this is all about. You should be asking the same kind of careful questions you would if you were buying a house or a car, and then some.

GENDER

Boys' Camps

Agawam
Carolina
Chewonki
Deerhorn
Dudley
Highlands
High Rocks
Keewaydin
Kieve
Killooleet
Pasquaney
Red Arrow
Timanous
Virginia
Winnebago
Winona

Girls' Camps

Alford Lake
Clearwater
Merrie-Woode
Onaway
Osoha
Red Pine
Rockbrook
Tapawingo
Waldemar
Wawenock
Wohelo
Wyonegonic

Coed Camps

Cape Cod Sea
Douglas Ranch
(separate programs)
Elk Creek Ranch
Farm & Wilderness
Gold Arrow
Hidden Valley
Interlochen Arts
Kingsley Pines
Longhorn
Tamarack Tennis
Windridge Tennis and Sports

Separate Camps

Aloha
Cheley Colorado
Clara Barton/Elliott Joslin
Farm & Wilderness
Mondamin and Green Cove
Sanborn Western
Seafarer/Seagull
Stewart/Heart O'the Hills
Susquehannock
Thunderbird

Separate Sessions

Camp Maxwelton/Lachlan
Teton Valley Ranch

CAMP COST

(not-for-profit camps designated by ★)

Camp	Weeks					
	2	3	3½	4	7	8
Agawam★			1800		3600	
Alford Lake			2500		3950	
Aloha Camps★			2575		4050	
Cape Cod Sea Camps		2550			4500	
Carolina	950	1350		1650		4500
Cheley Colorado		2300		2250	3950	
Chewonki★	950					
Clara Barton★	1000					
Elliott Joslin★						
Clearwater			1775		3300	3140 (9)
Deerhorn	950	1350		1800	2290 (6)	
Douglas Ranch	1450	2100		2550		
Dudley★				1850		3375
Elk Creek Ranch★				2350		3500
Farm & Wilderness★				2250		3600
Gold Arrow	1450	1850		2500			725 (1)
Hidden Valley				2495		4150
Highlands	1000	1400		1875	3100	
High Rocks	1025	1425		1875		3550
Interlochen★				2130		3650
Keewaydin★				2700		
Kieve★			2350		4700	
Killooleet						3700 (7½)
Kingsley Pines		1995			3595 (6)	

Camp	Fees
Lachlan	1055
Longhorn	1157, 1554
Maxwelton	1075
Merrie–Woode★	940, 1365, 1395 (5)
Mondamin/Green	2085 (5)
Cove	375 (1), 1450, 3100 (6½)
Onaway★	3350
Osoha	2150, 3300
Pasquaney★	3350
Red Arrow	3000
Red Pine	1665, 3280
Rockbrook	995, 1595
Sanborn Western	2350 (5)
Seafarer/Seagull★	400 (1), 1750
Stewart/Heart	1395 (2½), 1995
Susquehannock	1950, 2750 (6), 3500
Tamarack	1200, 2075
Tapawingo	2850, 4950
Teton Valley	2450 (5)
Thunderbird	2150, 3475
Timanous	2600, 3650
Virginia	700 (1), 1500, 2400 (6)
Waldemar	2300 (5)
Wawenock	3350
Windridge	1450–1600 (2½), 2800 (4½)
Winnebago	3100, 5150
Winona	2375, 3975
Wohelo	2450, 3800
Wyonegonic	2375, 3975

The Best Camps

CAMP LOCATION

Camp		Town/State
Agawam	6	Raymond, ME
Alford Lake Camp	2	Union, ME
Aloha Camps		
Aloha Hive	13	Fairlee, VT
Aloha Camp	13	Fairlee, VT
Camp Lanakila	13	Fairlee, VT
Cape Cod Sea Camps	21	Brewster, MA
Camp Carolina	29	Brevard, NC
Cheley Colorado Camps	40	Estes Park, CO
Camp Chewonki	4	Wiscasset, ME
Clara Barton Camp	20	North Oxford, MA
Elliott P. Joslin Camp	19	Charlton, MA
Clearwater Camp	34	Minocqua, WI
Deerhorn	33	Rhinelander, WI
Douglas Ranch Camps	45	Carmel Valley, CA
Camp Dudley YMCA	16	Westport, NY
Elk Creek Ranch and Trek Program	42	Cody, WY
Farm & Wilderness Camps	18	Plymouth, VT
Gold Arrow Camp	44	Lakeshore, CA
Hidden Valley Camp	1	Freedom, ME
Camp Highlands for Boys	32	Sayner, WI
Camp High Rocks	30	Cedar Mountain, NC
Interlochen Arts Camp	31	Interlochen, MI
Keewaydin Camps	17	Salisbury, VT
Camp Kieve	3	Nobleboro, ME
Killooleet	15	Hancock, VT
Kingsley Pines Camp	6	Raymond, ME
Camp Longhorn	39	Burnet, TX
Camp Maxwelton (for boys)	25	Rockbridge Baths, VA
Camp Lachlan (for girls)	25	Rockbridge Baths, VA
Camp Merrie-Woode	28	Sapphire, NC

GUIDE

Camp		Town/State
Camp Mondamin (for boys)	27	Tuxedo, NC
Green Cove (for girls)	27	Tuxedo, NC
Camp Onaway	11	Bristol, NH
Camp Osoha	36	Boulder Junction, WI
Pasquaney	11	Bristol, NH
Red Arrow	35	Woodruff, WI
Red Pine	34	Minocqua, WI
Rockbrook Camp	29	Brevard, NC
Sanborn Western Camps (Big Spring Ranch for boys and High Trail for girls)	41	Florissant, CO
Camp Seagull (for boys)	26	Arapahoe, NC
Camp Seafarer (for girls)	26	Arapahoe, NC
Camp Stewart (for boys)	38	Hunt, TX
Heart O'the Hills (for girls)	38	Hunt, TX
Susquehannock (for boys)	22	Brackney, PA
Susquehannock (for girls)	23	Friendsville, PA
Tamarack Tennis	12	Franconia, NH
Camp Tapawingo	9	Sweden, ME
Teton Valley Ranch	43	Kelly, WY
Camp Thunderbird (for boys)	37	Bemidji, MN
Camp Thunderbird (for girls)	37	Bemidji, MN
Camp Timanous	6	Raymond, ME
Camp Virginia	24	Goshen, VA
Camp Waldemar	38	Hunt, TX
Camp Wawenock	6	Raymond, ME
Windridge Tennis Camps	14	Craftsbury Common, VT
Camp Winnebago	7	Kents Hill, ME
Winona Camps	8	Bridgton, ME
Wohelo–Luther Gulick	5	South Casco, ME
Wyonegonic Camps	10	Denmark, ME

Agawam

Summer address:
54 Agawam Road
Raymond, Maine 04071

Phone:
(207) 627-4780

Winter address:
30 Fieldstone Lane
Hanover, MA 02339

Phone:
(617) 826-5913

Natural features:
Located on Crescent Lake, with forest and open areas

Nearest large city or town:
Portland, North Windham, Raymond

Enrollment:
Boys

Age spread:
8–15

Per summer:
125

Campers come from the:
Northeast 70% Southeast 5% Central 5% Northwest 5% Southwest 5% International 10%

Average number of international campers:
14—France 6, Japan 5, Switzerland 2

Season:
June 28–August 15

Session (by percentage of campers) and cost:
7 weeks, 95%, $3,600
3½ weeks, 5%, $1,800

Extra charges:
Some (uniforms, some trips)

Scholarships:
10% of campers do not pay full tuition

Financial structure:
Private, not for profit

Founded:
1919

Owner(s) and years associated with camp:
Agawam Council, 10

Managing Director(s) and years associated with camp:
Garth Nelson, 10

Director's background:
Garth Nelson: B.S., Cornell University; secondary school certification; eight years high school science teacher; 15 years high school varsity soccer coach; 15 years camper, counselor, waterfront and trips director, Camp Passumsic; Board of Directors, Maine Youth Camping Association, ACA, NE Section

Counselors: 40
Men 90% Women 10% Min. age 18
Ratio to campers 1: 3½

Health and safety:
RNs on staff; two local towns serve the camp with rescue units

Concentration:
Individual and team sports, tennis, swimming, sailing, handicrafts and creative arts,
camping, environment appreciation

Mission:
"To provide a happy, safe summer home for boys where the environment and activities will help
them grow physically, mentally, morally and spiritually. Agawam has long been recognized for its
belief in values clarification and upstanding moral character. An important guideline for our
community is to 'be all that you can be.' Significant effort is given to creating a group where
high standards of behavior, language, sportsmanship and awareness and concern for others are
valued and evident."

Agawam is located on Crescent Lake, north of Sebago Lake, in the lakes
region of south-central Maine. Comprising sixty-five acres and about two
thousand feet of lakefront, the campus sits upon a sunny hillside in a mixture of
pine forest and wide open fields.

The first thing you might notice upon entering the camp is how well the
property is put to use, both for its activities program and its aesthetics. The three
groups of living cabins and other buildings are located near the lake shore, surrounding a large open area in which most activities occur. The abundant back
acreage serves to isolate the campus from both the public access road and its neighbors.

This is a fine old camp in its seventy-third year, and many of its original
buildings, rustic as they are, have been superbly maintained. Governor Hall, the
general recreation building, contains a large stone fireplace, a small camp library
and reading area, open space for indoor activities, a performance stage, and a full-
length porch. Chapel is held here, and the walls are lined with photos of campers
from years gone by. A stone fireplace is also the centerpiece of the dining hall, a
spacious building with banners hanging from its rafters and large windows offering
a wide view of the camp. Separate buildings house arts and crafts, woodworking,
photography, and nature/campcraft classes.

Among Agawam's playing fields are a baseball diamond and small soccer field,
four tennis courts (two lighted for night play), and a fine asphalt basketball court.
The waterfront consists of a large sandy beach, wide H-dock for swimming instruction, and separate docking facilities for windsurfing, sailing, canoeing, and rowing.

The lake is warm and clear, and the beach bottom is sandy. Beyond the swimming area, where the bottom turns rocky, the boys go snorkeling and fishing. Campers change for waterfront activities in a covered boathouse adjacent to the beach.

Despite the abundance of fine facilities, there remains an uncomplicated feel to this place. Boys wear simple T-shirt-and-shorts uniforms and are, together with the entire staff, the most polite group of campers I have encountered in my travels.

Agawam boys enjoy a free-choice program of activities, but one with guidance from counselors, who encourage them—especially the younger ones—to strive for a balance among waterfront activities, land sports, creative arts, and outdoor-living skills. Most programs use a multilevel award system to monitor progress and encourage continued effort. And many of the sports activities (tennis, soccer, baseball, basketball, lacrosse, riflery, and archery) contain some element of competition, such as intracamp or intercamp league matches. Sailors attend weekly regattas as well as larger all-day meets on some of the local lakes.

Noncompetitive activities include arts and crafts, camping (incorporating the Junior Maine Guide Program), canoeing, dramatics, Indian lore, basic rescue and water safety, nature study, newspaper and yearbook, swimming, diving, backpacking and canoe trips, photography, snorkeling, windsurfing, and wood shop.

Agawam places a greater emphasis on character development and values clarification than do most camps. High standards are set for behavior, character, sportsmanship, leadership, and mutual respect. To focus those goals, the camp has employed a unique system, called "katiaki," since the early 1930s. Each week the staff assigns each camper a personal katiaki—that is, a goal related to some aspect of his character, or maybe to a particular skill in dealing with others, or to various other life challenges. During the week, members of the staff individually provide feedback to the camper, and at the end of the week, the staff collectively determines whether he has striven enough to attain his katiaki goal (the emphasis is on *effort*). If so, he is rewarded publicly at the weekly council fire.

Traditions like katiaki mean a lot at Agawam. From the stalwart appearance of the camp and campers to the boys' exemplary and genuine behavior, high energy, and enthusiasm, this camp stands firmly in league with what the finest American camps have been all about for a hundred years. Ghost rocks, Hiawatha's departure, flags and totems, council fires, Indian feathers—these things all have deep meaning to an old camper like me, as they do to the boys at Agawam.

Alford Lake Camp

Summer address:
RR 2, Box 6360
Union, Maine 04862

Phone:
(207) 785-2400

Winter address:
17 Pilot Point Road
Cape Elizabeth, ME 04107

Phone:
(207) 799-3005

Natural features:
Situated on Lake Alford, 100 acres of woods and blueberry fields; close proximity to mountains and seacoast

Nearest large city or town:
Between Rockland and Augusta

Enrollment:
Girls (co-ed trips)

Age spread:
8–15

Per summer:
175

Campers come from the:
Northeast 58% Southeast 19% Central 6% Northwest 4% Southwest 3% International 10%

Average number of international campers (21 countries represented):
Estonia 5, Komi 5, Spain 5, France 4, Mexico 4, Colombia 3, Venezuela 3, Austria 2, England 2

Season:
June 27–August 14

Session (by percentage of campers) and cost:
3½ weeks, 55%, $2,500
7 weeks, 45%, $3,950

Extra charges:
7-week special trips are separately priced

Scholarships:
15% of campers do not pay full tuition

Financial structure:
For profit

Founded:
1907

Owner(s) and years associated with camp:
Jean G. McMullan, 32
Sue S. McMullan, 25

Managing Director(s) and years associated with camp:
Jean G. McMullan, 32
Sue S. McMullan, 25

Other Director(s) and years associated with camp:
Mark A. McMullan, 13

Directors' backgrounds:
Jean G. McMullan: B.A., M.A., music, guidance; Certified Camp Director (ACA); Past National ACA President

Sue S. McMullan: B.A., University of
Maine; college basketball coach; EMT on
Cape Rescue Squad; Certified ACA Camp
Director

Mark A. McMullan: business executive,
camp co-director

Counselors: 60
Men 5% Women 95% Min. age 18
Ratio to campers 1: 3

Health and safety:
Infirmary, 2 RNs on staff; doctor on call;
several Emergency Medical Technicians
(EMTs) and Advanced First Aiders (AFAs)
on staff; hospital nearby

Concentration:
Trip and Trail Program (campcraft and canoeing); mountain climbing; swimming, riding, sailing, sailboarding; creative and
performing arts

Mission:
 "Alford Lake Camp believes that campers should experience both challenge and adventure
through a broad program that is largely elective on a daily basis for each camper. A camper
should feel warm acceptance of herself as she is and, at the same time, a steady encouragement to
improve in constructive ways."

Alford Lake Camp is spread over more than four hundred acres of Maine
blueberry fields and woods, featuring a mile of shoreline on a large spring-
fed lake. The campus is situated in one of the nicest spots in Maine, within ten
miles of the ocean, and close to many mountains and rivers as well. This is one of
those places that *feels* right the moment you arrive, and nothing about the campus
diminishes that feeling. The atmosphere is always happy and busy, and almost everyone you meet acts like an old friend.

Since its founding in 1907, Alford Lake Camp has progressed considerably from
a small, Boston/New York-oriented camp of seventy campers to one that serves a
diverse group of two hundred girls from about twenty-six states and twenty-one
foreign countries. In 1987 the camp was distinguished by being selected as the first
camp, in conjunction with the Samantha Smith Foundation, for the landmark So-
viet/American exchange of campers between the two countries. Today the Alford
Lake/Russian exchange is well integrated into the camp program.

Facilities are numerous here and are kept in excellent condition. There are
several grassy playing fields, a sandy beach, four all-weather tennis courts, several
woodland trails for the camp's thirteen horses, and a large gymnastics area, as well
as a campfire area and a chapel in the pines for Sunday services.

A large farmhouse contains the dining hall, camp offices, and recreation space.

There are also a general recreation hall with a stage and two fireplaces; a health center; three art buildings; a large stable with two riding rings; a new counselor-recreation building; a music building; a library; a nature building; several staff living cabins; shower and toilet buildings; and areas for sailing, canoeing, and sailboarding. Campers sleep in thirty-nine roomy platform tents, six, plus a counselor, to a tent.

Alford Lake girls are separated into eight age groups for activities. In keeping with the camp's underlying mission to teach responsible decision-making and life skills, the selection of activities is largely free choice, from a menu of three basic programs: Lifetime Sports, the Arts, and Nature and Wilderness.

Lifetime Sports include horseback riding, swimming, sailing, sailboarding, canoeing, gymnastics, tennis, archery, and kayaking, as well as team games such as soccer, softball, basketball, lacrosse, and field hockey.

The Arts involve a variety of projects in drawing, painting, clay, photography, pottery, ceramics, and crafts. Singing, poetry reading, gymnastics, and dance (the girls choreograph their own routines) are all activities that go on continuously and reflect Alford Lake's commitment to cultural values. Short plays are presented weekly, and each summer the camp performs a major Broadway or well-known play.

The Nature and Wilderness program brings into play canoeing, campcraft, and exploration skills, and provides the basis for many ambitious river, lake, mountain, and ocean trips. Over forty trips leave camp each summer, not counting some of the camp's challenging seven-week special trips, which include touring Great Britain or traveling through America's West. Several coed trips, offered in conjunction with Maine's Camp Chewonki, include hiking and backpacking the Appalachian Trail from Mt. Katahdin to the White Mountains of New Hampshire; or canoeing, kayaking, and sailing in Maine's rivers and ocean (see Camp Chewonki for details).

Trips aside, there are always plenty of opportunities for a change of pace from daily activities. For example, every week the entire camp spends a day at the seacoast, swimming, exploring, or just relaxing. And evenings are lively with entertainment, from scavenger hunts and "paper bag" dramatics to song contests.

Alford Lake Camp is both an idealistic community, devoted to international peace and understanding, and a carefully managed, stable institution. It's a camp that truly practices what it preaches, making it easy to get beyond the superficial differences that separate people to a place where human nature is universal.

On the wall of the dining hall is a plaque awarded by the leading international exchange group in recognition of Alford Lake's role in initiating camper exchanges between America and Russia. The plaque reads: "The *Druzhba* [friendship] Award honors the camp which has done the most to improve international understanding between the Soviet Union and the American people." From what I have seen here, a world that attempts to live as these girls do would be a world at peace.

Aloha Camps

Aloha Hive for Girls, ages 7–12
Aloha Camp for Girls, ages 12–17
Camp Lanakila for Boys, ages 8–14

Summer address:
Aloha Hive
RR 1, Box 289
Fairlee, Vermont 05045

Aloha Camp
RR 1, Box 91B
Fairlee, Vermont 05045

Camp Lanakila
RR 1, Box 98
Fairlee, Vermont 05045

Phone:
Aloha Hive: (802) 333-4337
Aloha Camp: (802) 333-4355
Camp Lanakila: (802) 333-9766

Winter address:
Aloha Hive
RR 1, Box 91A
Fairlee, VT 05045

Aloha Camp
Route 4, Box 30A
Chester, VT 05143

Camp Lanakila
PO Box 104
Norwich, VT 05055

Phone:
Aloha Hive: (802) 875-3074
Aloha Camp: (802) 875-3074
Camp Lanakila: (802) 649-2135
or (802) 333-9113

Natural features:
Located on lakes, with woods and open
spaces; close to mountains

Nearest large city or town:
Between Hanover, NH, and Bradford, VT

Enrollment:
Girls and boys

Age spread:
7–17

Per summer:
Each camp: 125–170

Campers come from the:
Northeast 60% Southeast 10% Central 10%
Southwest 5% Northwest 5% International
10%

*Average number of international
campers:*
15—France 5, Japan 3, Mexico 2

Season:
June 28–August 16

*Session (by percentage of campers)
and cost:*
3¹⁄₂ weeks, 35%, $2,575
7 weeks, 65%, $4,050

Extra charges:
Some (riding, tutoring)

Scholarships:
15% of campers do not pay full tuition

Financial structure:
Private, not-for-profit educational
foundation

Founded:
1905

Owner(s) and years associated with camp:
The Aloha Foundation, Inc., 23

Manager(s) and years associated with camp:
Posie Merritt Taylor, 36

Director(s) and years associated with camp:
Aloha Hive
Helen Rankin Butler, 10

Aloha Camp
Nancy L. Pennell, 41

Camp Lanakila
Dr. Barnes Boffey, 31

Directors' backgrounds:
Helen Rankin Butler: graduate, Yale University; teacher

Nancy L. Pennell: B.A., University of Mississippi

Dr. Barnes Boffey: graduate, Middlebury College; Ph.D. in education, University of Massachusetts; former teacher at elementary and college levels; maintains private practice in individual and family counseling

Counselors:
    Aloha Hive—74
Men 5% Women 95% Min. age 18
Ratio to campers 1: 2
    Aloha Camp—66
Men 6% Women 94% Min. age 18
Ratio to campers 1: 2½
    Camp Lanakila—40
Men 89% Women 11% Min. age 18
Ratio to campers 1: 2½

Health and safety:
Infirmary, RN on staff; doctor on call; hospital nearby

Concentration:
Swimming, trips and outdoor skills; biking, hiking, and canoeing in the Green and White mountains

Mission:
"We believe that having fun means achieving success, meeting challenges, and the satisfaction of knowing you are an effective member of a group. The lasting life skills developed at camp include self-confidence, group cooperation, and the ability to cope resourcefully and responsibly with the challenges of independent living."

These three camps are separately located in east-central Vermont between the Green Mountains and New Hampshire's White Mountains. Aloha and Lanakila are a mile apart on adjacent shores of Lake Morey, with Aloha Hive seven miles away, on Lake Fairlee. Together, the camps comprise nearly a thousand acres of wooded hills, open fields, and lake shore. Facilities are excellent throughout; buildings are well aged and impeccably maintained, and fields are kept in excellent condition.

These are camps that strive to be noncompetitive, emphasizing community building, self-esteem, and confidence. Campers and counselors alike wear a simple camp uniform, which, in the words of the camp brochure, "reduces social barriers and simplifies the issue of what is and what is not appropriate dress." But fashion is the last thing on these youngsters' minds. If you close your eyes at any of these camps, you'll hear the same sounds—of happy, energetic kids having fun.

Aloha offers campers a lot of choice in the selection of their activities. While the program is slightly more structured for the youngest campers, the oldest may decide to concentrate on only one or two favorite activities. Flexibility is built into the program in other ways as well. The girls of Aloha may take one- and two-week workshops in field hockey, dance, photography, and tennis, or they may take those activities as one of many daily offerings, which include archery, sailing (with weekly races with Lanakila, all-day sails, and a tri-camp regatta), swimming, lake and white-water canoeing, campcraft, a wide range of arts and crafts, ropes course, riflery, horseback riding, music, and a fine drama program, which oversees the production of a professional-quality musical each season. Aloha also has an extensive tripping program, with biking, hiking, and canoeing trips (some trips are coed) traveling into the Green and White mountains as well as to the Adirondacks and up into Maine.

The younger girls of Aloha Hive live in small tent clusters, three girls plus a counselor to each tent. Their activities are similar to those of the older Aloha girls, but with a more routine schedule, and their tripping program is suitably less ambitious.

Lanakila boys live in four separate units, divided by age, each with its own clubhouse, wash house, and playing fields. Among the optional activities offered these boys are sailing, boating, archery, riflery, tennis, riding, crafts, photography, shop, athletics (baseball, soccer, basketball, track, football, volleyball), tripping, campcraft, exploring, biking, hiking, dramatics (featuring a major musical production), canoeing, a superb ropes course (with spider web and zip wire), and swimming (with swim teams, water polo, a snorkeling club, and swim trips). Lanakila offers its campers a series of honors called Viking Awards, which represent the Lanakila motto of "victory over oneself." All three camps offer short introductory programs for first-time campers.

Aloha is a wonderfully managed, secure educational institution that really delivers on its mission. And the camp's financial structure—a not-for-profit educational foundation with a self-perpetuating board of trustees—guarantees its endurance for a long time to come. The educational value of the camps has been further en-hanced by the 1978 addition of the Hubert Outdoor Center, a nature-education institution that runs year-round for groups of all ages.

This is a heartfelt camp whose counselors and directors know each of their campers inside out. At a nearly two-to-one camper-to-staff ratio (the lowest I've seen), these boys and girls enjoy close personal relationships with the staff and with one another, which may best explain why both campers and counselors are so anxious to get back here year after year.

Cape Cod Sea Camps

Address:
P.O. Box 1880
Brewster, Massachusetts 02631

Phone:
(508) 896-3451 or (508) 896-3832
Fax (508) 896-8272

Contact person:
David L. Peterson or Sherry Mernick

Natural features:
Situated on 1,000 feet of sandy beach on Cape Cod Bay. The 50-acre campus also includes a fresh water pond, estuaries, tidal flats, and a lily pond, plus a 70-acre outpost on Long Pond.

Nearest large city or town:
Hyannis

Enrollment:
Coed
Boys 46% Girls 54%

Age spread:
7–15 (16–17 returns only)

Per summer:
320

Campers come from the:
Northeast 70% Southeast 6% Central 6% Northwest 2% Southwest 2% International 14%

Average number of international campers:
Mexico 12, France 11, Switzerland 8, Kuwait 4, England 3, Germany 3, Italy 3, Japan 3, Spain 2

Season:
July 2–August 18

Session (by percentage of campers) and cost:
3 weeks, $2,550
7 weeks, $4,500

Extra charges:
optional trips ($40–$65)
camp services ($100–$200)

Scholarships:
5% of campers do not pay full tuition

Financial structure:
For profit

Founded:
1922

Owner(s) and years associated with camp:
Frances Delahanty Garran, 66 (lifetime)
Berry Delahanty Richardson (lifetime)
Carol Austin, Mary Jane Collins

Manager and years associated with camp:
Frank Lajoie, 24

Director(s) and years associated with camp:
David Peterson, 24
Sherry Mernick, 25
Nancy Garran, 25

Directors' backgrounds:
David Peterson: B.S., Southern Connecticut State University; Past President ACA, NE

Section; member of numerous ACA committees; teacher in Cape Cod and Australia

Sherry Mernick: B.S., Skidmore College; M.Ed., Northeastern University; Secretary, Cape Cod Association of Children's Camps; serves on numerous ACA committees; schoolteacher in Vermont

Nancy Garran: RN, B.S., CCD; granddaughter of camp founder

Counselors: 76
Men 48% Women 52% Min. age 19
Ratio to campers 1: 4

Health and Safety:
Infirmary, 4 RNs on staff, part-time pediatrician; medical center five miles away

Concentration:
Strong waterfront activities, sailing, swimming, tennis, athletics, gymnastics, woodworking, performing and fine arts, archery, riflery, windsurfing

Mission:
"A safe, educational, happy experience. Each camper should come away from camp with the tangible evidence of having succeeded in an activity, as well as the intangible feelings of self-esteem, self-worth and self-confidence. Friendship, respect, generosity in sharing, open communications and trust are among the values used each day."

This is one of those places that just can't miss. Besides having a first-rate administration and staff and a sound educational philosophy, Cape Cod Sea Camps is located on a private Cape Cod beach, surrounded by about sixty acres of coastal woodland. If that's not enough, the camp also owns a separate outpost facility three miles away on the Cape's largest lake, where campers spend overnights, swim, water-ski, windsurf, canoe, and sail.

Facilities throughout are extensive and of high quality, indicative of the care that is given the entire operation. There are eight acres of level, grassy playing fields, including two full-size fields for football and soccer, plus baseball and softball diamonds, and fine archery and riflery ranges, nine tennis courts, and a basketball court. Other facilities include woodworking and crafts shops, a large, open-air pavilion for gymnastics and dance, an outdoor theater with enclosed stage and prop-storage area, and a ten-element low ropes course.

As its name might imply, Cape Cod Sea Camps has a special commitment to waterfront activities. Both ocean and lake beaches are sandy and clean and always teeming with water sports and lessons. For rainy days, there are two large indoor areas for sailing instruction. Swimming is taught in the camp's large, four-lane fresh-water pool.

Campers are grouped into units of 30 according to age, grade, maturity, and friendships, and they stay in cabins that are adjoined by toilet and shower facilities. Each unit has its own head counselor and staff, augmented by junior counselor assistants (who are enrolled in the camp's four-year Junior Counselor Program, for ages fourteen to seventeen).

Activities are coed, with boys and girls grouped together according to age or skill levels. Although swimming is mandatory for all campers, boys and girls may choose the rest of their program from a list of activities that includes sailing, tennis, archery, riflery, dramatics, arts and crafts, hiking, woodworking, waterskiing, windsurfing, canoeing, nature, adventure ropes course, and a variety of team sports. Sailing, the camp's most popular activity, is taken for either the entire morning or afternoon period so that the campers can get the most out of the lesson. For those who want competition, there are intracamp team sports, tennis matches, swimming meets, and sailing races.

To help build confidence, campers here are encouraged to make some kind of presentation in front of a group. Every morning, for example, a different cabin is responsible for the morning assembly, which entails discussing the news or daily events and singing or leading group songs. On Sunday evenings campers perform in a weekly variety show.

The people here and the way they work with one another are what makes this place as good as it is. Campers feel wanted, and so do the staff people. It's almost second nature to these people to offer a warm welcome whenever somebody new arrives at camp, or even when one of their own enters a room. Alumni who return after having been away for fifty or sixty years notice that the camp's energy is still expended on the same essential values: "the guidance of youth, the principles of love, and an appreciation of God's world and people."

Staff and campers both come away from this place with a deep appreciation of how people gain from a close-knit, intensive community effort. This is an institution that works very well because everybody feels an important part of the team, and everybody is encouraged constantly. If, for some reason, somebody forgets, the camp motto is posted above the stage for all to see: "I can, and I will."

Camp Carolina

Address:
Box 552
Brevard, North Carolina 28712

Phone:
(704) 884-2414

Natural features:
Bordering mountainous Pisgah National Forest, and enclosing a 4½-acre spring-fed lake

Nearest large city or town:
South of Asheville

Enrollment:
Boys

Age spread:
7–16

Per summer:
700

Campers come from the:
Northeast 2% Southeast 85% Central 5% Southwest 5% International 3%

Average number of international campers:
15—Mexico 3, France 2, Germany 2, Spain 2

Season:
June 11–August 20

Session (by percentage of campers) and cost:
2 weeks*, 33%, $950
3 weeks, 33%, $1,350
4 weeks, 33%, $1,650

Scholarships:
2% of campers do not pay full tuition

Extra charges:
Very few

Financial structure:
For profit

Founded:
1924

Owner(s) and years associated with camp:
Thompson family, 36

Managing Director(s) and years associated with camp:
Nath Thompson, 36

Other Director(s) and years associated with camp:
Mary B. Thompson, 11
Charles N. Thompson, Jr., 15
Alfred B. Thompson, 8

Directors' backgrounds:
Nath Thompson: B.A., University of Georgia; former camper, camp counselor, business manager; 36 years director of Camp Carolina

Mary B. Thompson: camp secretary and office manager

Charles N. Thompson, Jr.: camper, counselor, assistant director

Alfred B. Thompson: M.S., North Carolina State University; camper, counselor, business manager

* The 2-week session is offered to a younger group of boys (6–12) who may prefer a shorter camp stay. The 3- and 4-week sessions are for boys 8–16.

Counselors: 60
Men 92% Women 8% Min. age 18
Ratio to campers 1: 4

Health and safety:
Infirmary, 2 RNs on staff; doctor and hospital 2½ miles away

Concentration:
High adventure on rocks, woods, water, and trail; team sports, individual sports, crafts, and nature

Mission:
"Our philosophy centers around simplicity of life, self-reliance, human relations, wonders of nature, and high adventure. Emphasis is on good citizenship in all phases of camp life."

Camp Carolina sits in the middle of a half-million acres of national forest. Although its 224-acre campus is extremely well maintained, the property manages to retain the natural beauty of its surroundings, cut through with a clear mountain stream and miles of well-worn horse trails, with four trails leading into Pisgah Forest up to elevations of six thousand feet.

The campus includes twenty-five acres of grass fields, a trout pond in the woods, and a swimming lake that is fed by sixteen separate springs. Facilities are extremely well kept, with fields for soccer, football, baseball, and lacrosse, a golf driving range, and riding rings. One of the unique features of this camp is its hang-glider trainer. From a cable at Dining Hall Hill, campers are secured into a vest and then soar to a safe landing in the valley below. Another confidence builder is the zip line, which runs over the lake from a thirty-foot tower to the shore on the other side.

This is a happy, adventuresome camp whose campers and counselors seem to love being here. Each camper is given his own bunk bed, a locker for his clothes, and a place for his trunk. The cabins are screened, with commanding views of the campus. Each age group has its own lodge for meetings, evening programs, and rainy-day activities.

Camp Carolina offers seventeen activities five periods per day, as well as five tripping activities. Campers choose between two or three activities for each of the five periods. The following week they are given the opportunity to repeat the same activities or try some new ones, as they wish. At almost any time campers may break from their in-camp activities to go on trips, either by volunteering or being invited to go.

Featured activities are tennis, on six hard-surface lakeside courts; golf, with a driving range, practice nets, and trips twice a week to area golf courses; water sports, with emphasis on American Red Cross water safety; diving, from a one-meter board and a high dive; and riflery (medals and certificates from the NRA). Other sports include soccer, basketball, football, baseball, and wrestling.

For the boys who pass swim tests and work on their canoeing skills in the lake, there are white-water river trips. Once a boy has demonstrated horseback skills in the riding rings, he may go on overnight and day rides into Pisgah Forest. There are also opportunities for white-water rafting, deep-woods camping, and, for the older boys, rock climbing and rappelling.

Camp Carolina strives for a balance of team sports, individual sports, crafts, nature, and tripping activities. Competition is played down by avoiding permanent teams and competition with other camps. The emphasis is not on competition, or even achievement, but on citizenship. In fact, there is only one award given by Camp Carolina, and that is the Good Citizenship Award.

On Friday night all campers and counselors gather at the campfire across the lake for singing, stories, and recognition ceremonies. On Sundays there are religious services, free time for letter writing and reading, and special games in the afternoon, capped off by an evening vesper service at the outdoor chapel at the end of the lake.

Carolina is a lively place, powered by a sort of structured informality. The air around the campus sings with the sounds of loudspeaker announcements, often with sounds of boys' laughter. Even meals are noisy and informal, despite the obvious care that goes into feeding the boys. "Our dietitian/food manager plans a balanced diet every day," says director Nath Thompson, "with emphasis on *quantity*." There are three big meals per day, a fruit break at midmorning, and a "health food store," where campers can purchase nutritious snacks.

Safety and health are important at Carolina, emphasized to the staff at their four-and-a-half-day orientation and to the campers throughout their stay. A health card on each camper is kept by the boy's cabin counselor and sent home to his parents each week. A pediatrician visits twice each week, and there is always at least one nurse on campus. All trips out of camp include at least two counselors, one twenty-one years old or older.

Camp Carolina and its directors have been around for a long time, and it shows.

Everything about this environment instills a quiet confidence. "Our purpose," states Thompson, "is to make the boys' summer a valuable factor in their complete development. Carolina is a camp where boys learn to see with their eyes, feel with their hearts, do with their hands, and live together in the spirit of brotherhood. A special effort is made to send every boy back home stronger in body, keener in mind, more appreciative of beauty, and nobler in character."

Cheley Colorado Camps, Inc.

Summer address:
P.O. Box 1170
Estes Park, Colorado 80517-1170

Phone:
(303) 586-4244
Fax (303) 586-3020

Winter address:
P.O. Box 6525
Denver, CO 80206-0525

Phone:
(303) 377-3616
Fax (303) 377-3605

Natural features:
8,000-foot elevation, adjacent to Rocky Mountain National Park; streams and creeks running through campus

Nearest large city or town:
Boulder, Loveland

Enrollment:
Coed
Boys 50% Girls 50%

Age spread:
9–17

Per summer:
952

Campers come from the:
Northeast 4% Southeast 12% Central 24% Northwest 4% Southwest 50% International 6%

Average number of international campers:
36—Mexico 20, France 5, England 3, Germany 2, Hong Kong 2, Japan 2, Switzerland 2

Season:
June 19–August 12

Session (by percentage of campers) and cost:
4 weeks, 90%, $2,250
8 weeks, 10%, $4,500

Extra charges:
Some (personal laundry, camp store)

Scholarships:
2% of campers do not pay full tuition

Financial structure:
For profit

Founded:
1922

Owner(s) and years associated with camp:
Cheley family, 75

Managing Director(s) and years associated with camp:
Don Cheley, 51
Carole T. Cheley, 12

Directors' backgrounds:
Don Cheley: B.A., business administration

Carole T. Cheley: B.A., art education; master's in psychology; former elementary school counselor

Counselors: 187
Men 50% Women 50% Min. age 19
Ratio to Campers 1: 3

Health and safety:
4 infirmaries, 5 RNs on staff; hospital in
town

Concentration:
Noncompetitive; backpacking, mountaineering, western riding, nature, river rafting,
technical climbing; also sports, arts and
crafts, challenge course, wilderness
study

Mission:
"To inculcate in boys and girls that spirit of honesty, purity, unselfishness, love, alertness,
determination and courage which is the foundation for all that is big and fine in American life
and character; we aim to cultivate the ability to act spontaneously in the right, and by doing this
contribute definitely to the creation of a better world."

This is an expansive and beautifully maintained property, comfortably housing
six separate camps within its boundaries. The sound of streams and brooks
winding through the campus becomes a constant reminder of nature at work here,
while pines and aspens and the endless mountains of Rocky Mountain National
Park look down from all around.

The care that is given this place is evident the minute you enter the grounds,
passing beneath the lofty wooden arch, and nothing about Cheley will dispel that
first impression. Buildings throughout are constructed of wood and stone, in a
deliberate attempt to preserve the aesthetics of the environment. The dining room
is particularly attractive, featuring a fireplace and china bearing the camp logo.
There is a large recreation building for indoor tennis, basketball, and volleyball. The
main office is a highly professional building, yet, like so much of this place, it is
graced with pleasantries such as the baskets of flowers hanging on the porch or the
sign that reads "If you aren't as close to God as you once were, guess who moved?"

Cheley is essentially a western camp emphasizing western riding, spectacular
hiking and camping trips (overnight trips of two to five days), and technical climbing. Recognizing that some campers may prefer a concentrated riding experience,
Cheley offers two riding camps, in two different locations: The Land O' Peaks
Ranch Camps and The Trail's End Ranches, which is a specialized horsemanship
program.

The Land O' Peaks Ranch Camps are divided into two separate programs, one
for boys and one for girls, ages 7–17. Boys' and girls' camps are further divided by

age into three separate camps, each with its own distinct program and its own director, counselors, and assistants. And each has its own lodge for evening activities and rainy-day play. Boys share a common dining room, as do girls. Boys and girls occasionally join together for Sunday inspirational services and for occasional evening programs.

The Trail's End Ranches, for boys and girls ages twelve to seventeen, provide a western ranch type of camping experience and are divided into separate boys' and girls' camps. A unique feature here is that while Land O' Peaks campers sleep in cabins for ten to sixteen campers and counselors, Trail's End campers sleep in specially constructed covered wagons, four to a wagon, with counselors in adjacent cabins. Rustic though it may seem, the wagons are equipped with a drawer and hanging space for each camper, as well as innerspring mattresses.

Activities at Cheley are free choice but carefully balanced. No activity is required, although every effort is made to encourage campers to participate in everything the camp has to offer. Campers have the opportunity each week to choose their first and second preference for each day's activity, with directors and cabin counselors making sure that all campers have a fair chance at all programs. Activities include riflery, archery, handicrafts, sports, games, woodcrafts, motor trips, fly-fishing, and a challenge course. The camp does not offer a water program.

The only competition at Cheley is of the individual sort—against one's own previous best, and even then encouragement and enjoyment is the rule, not winning. Awards are given for good camping skills, good citizenship, and good attitude.

Here at Cheley, the entire staff, from barn hand to cook to counselor to director, is noticeably well organized and devoted to the mission. The staff seems to know their campers intimately, as if they were members of their own families.

It's no accident that one of the centerpieces of this camp is a large open-air chapel looking across the valley to a beautiful mountain range. Cheley is a community that is brought together to revere natural beauty, learn to care for one another, and build self-confidence—and it works that way. As the camp motto so aptly puts it, "Great things happen when youth and mountains meet."

Camp Chewonki

Address:
Chewonki Foundation, Inc.
RR 2, Box 1200
Wiscasset, Maine 04578

Phone:
(207) 882-7323

Natural features:
Situated on a peninsula in Montsweag Bay on the Maine seacoast, walking distance from a tidal salt waterfront

Nearest large city or town:
Between Bath and Rockland

Enrollment:
The camp is for boys; most trips are coed

Age spread:
8–18

Per summer:
350

Campers come from the:
Northeast 73% Southeast 7% Central 3% Northwest 2% Southwest 2% International 13%

Average number of international campers:
35—France 11, Italy 5, Russia 4, Germany 3, Spain 3, Austria 2

Season:
June 27–August 14

Session (by percentage of campers) and cost:
3 weeks, 60%, $2,300
7 weeks, 40%, $3,950

Extra charges:
Some (camp T-shirts)

Scholarships:
18% of campers do not pay full tuition

Financial structure:
Private, not for profit

Founded:
1915

Owner(s) and years associated with camp:
Chewonki Foundation, Inc., 32

Managing Director(s) and years associated with camp:
Dick Thomas, 24

Other Director(s) and years associated with camp:
Don Hudson, Executive Director, 27
Greg Shute, Wilderness Trip Director, 11
Peter Hamblin, 7

Directors' backgrounds:
Dick Thomas: B.A., University of Maine; five years director, five years assistant director, board member; Maine Youth Camping Association, ACA/NE

Don Hudson: A.B., Dartmouth; Ph.D., Indiana University

Greg Shute: B.S., University of Maine, Presque Isle

Peter Hamblin: B.A., Hamilton; Ph.D., University of Rochester; Dean of Studies, Waynflete School

Counselors: 35
Men 95% Women 5% Min. age 17
Ratio to campers 1: 4

Concentration:
Nature study; activities include sports, arts,
farming, and kayaking

Health and safety:
Infirmary, 2 RNs on staff; family nurse-
practitioner and doctor on call; hospital
nearby

Mission:
"Personal growth—not just in new skills and interests but in self-confidence, self-reliance and
personal integrity; a sense of community, and a sensitivity to the natural world."

Chewonki is located on a four-hundred-acre peninsula in mid-coast Maine,
surrounded by tidal bays, inlets, and salt marsh. It's a lively place; everywhere you look, people seem to be deeply involved in some activity or another,
whether playing volleyball, hoeing weeds from the garden, or huddling around a
snake somebody has discovered. The mark of a good camp is a clear mission, and
Chewonki's mission is about as clear as they come. This is an ecologically based
educational camp, and if learning were always this much fun, this would be a world
of very intelligent folks.

The special emphasis here is on exploring and understanding natural history
and ecology, implemented with lots of trips—by canoe, kayak, and sailboat, or up
the sides of mountains. The entire staff is dedicated to the appreciation of the
natural world around them. In fact, every program of this fine old camp is aimed in
the same direction—sustaining the fragile beauties of nature and promoting traditional, enduring values.

Because Chewonki is used as an educational facility during winter months,
buildings and grounds are exceptional, set off by gardens and patches of wildflowers. A new, winterized dining room offers family-style meals that are prepared
with nutrition in mind. Flags on the walls represent the home countries of all
Chewonki's campers. Other facilities that bear mentioning are an excellent indoor
ropes course and an extensive new waterfront dock.

The camp offers plenty of activities such as swimming, tennis, field sports,
archery, art, woodworking, and photography, as well as a terrific program in or-
ganic gardening and farming. And the program is rounded out with various service

projects and clubs for singing, rock climbing and rappelling, astronomy, and drama, as well as special events like sailing races, skit nights, carnivals, scavenger hunts, evening dips, campfires, folk singing, star watching, chess, checkers, and drama.

Chewonki boys stay in rustic cabins with six to nine other campers and a counselor. Cabin groups go on overnights and wilderness trips together and, as a group, offer contributions to campfires, talent shows, and other special events.

Learning to work together is an important part of the education at this camp, as is international friendship and cooperation. Chewonki, together with Alford Lake Camp, sponsors an exchange program with Russia for thirteen- and fourteen-year-olds, in which the camps host Russian campers and send five of their own campers and a counselor to visit Russia.

The activities program is divided into four groups, according to age:

Puffins (8–9) try all of the activities and go on a two-day wilderness trip to Camden Hills each three-week session. Seven-week Puffins may select certain activities on which to concentrate during the final session.

Owls (10–11) and Herons (12–13) are exposed to all of the activities but choose only a certain few so that they can make progress in those areas. Campers from each cabin spend several nights at an out-of-camp campsite, practicing their wilderness skills. These campers go on at least one trip of up to seven days.

Ospreys (13–15) follow a more challenging program of wilderness trips combined with in-camp activities. A nine-day sailing/rowing or canoeing trip is offered early in the summer, followed by a nine-day backpacking trip toward the end of the summer. In camp, Ospreys are offered a refined schedule of activities that may include lean-to building, trail maintenance, boat building, or other tasks. The Ospreys are expected to take a mature interest in their own growth and to provide leadership to younger campers.

Chewonki places great emphasis on small-group wilderness trips. As their brochure explains: "After an extended period of time in close contact with the reality of the natural world, campers learn to look at themselves and their world and distinguish between what is real and meaningful and what may be superfluous and self-indulgent."

In keeping with that philosophy, the camp offers an ambitious coed wilderness tripping program for boys and (Alford Lake) girls, ages fourteen to eighteen. Each trip has ten participants and two leaders. The trips include Umbagog, a seven-week white-water, kayaking, and wilderness-living trip; Thoreau Wilderness Trip, seven weeks of canoeing and hiking in northern Maine; Mariner, a three-and-a-half-week exploration of the Maine coast in traditional wooden sailing/rowing boats; Downeast Sea Kayaking, a three-and-a-half-week exploration of the Maine coast in seagoing kayaks; Mistassin, five weeks of canoeing with a Cree Indian guide in the northern Canadian wilderness; and Boat Building/Exploration, three weeks of building a sea kayak, followed by three and a half weeks on expedition.

In addition, Chewonki boys may go with Alford Lake Camp girls on special seven-week trips, including an Appalachian Trail hike, or tours of the British Isles or American West (see "Alford Lake Camp" for more details).

Chewonki is a special place filled with extra-special people who are single-mindedly dedicated to their environmental mission. Even the camp's entrance road speaks the language: Large pine forests on either side are carefully managed to retain their value; frequent signs remind travelers to go slow; other signs say NO HUNTING. This is a well-managed, confident institution that earns every bit of its fine reputation and will endure for years to come.

Clara Barton Camp for Girls with Diabetes, Inc.

Elliott P. Joslin Camp for Boys with Diabetes

Summer address:
Clara Barton Camp
P.O. Box 356
68 Clara Barton Road
North Oxford, Massachusetts
01537-0356

Elliott P. Joslin Camp
Box 100
Charlton, Massachusetts 01507

Phone:
Clara Barton Camp: (508) 987-2056
Camp Joslin: (617) 248-5220

Winter address:
Clara Barton Camp
P.O. Box 356
68 Clara Barton Road
North Oxford, MA
01537-0356

Elliott P. Joslin Camp
Joslin Diabetes Center
1 Joslin Place
Boston, MA 02215

Phone:
Clara Barton Camp: same
Camp Joslin: (617) 732-2455

Contact person:
Clara Barton Camp: Shelley D. Yeager or Kassie Gregono

Camp Joslin: Paul Madden, Julie Spataro, or Bob Gannon

Natural features:
Clara Barton Camp: 125 wooded acres; pond; hiking trails

Camp Joslin: 300 acres of woods and fields; 20-acre pond; additional oceanfront site on Cape Cod

Nearest large city or town:
Both camps between Worcester and Sturbridge

Enrollment:
Clara Barton Camp: Girls
(Coed family weekends in off-season)

Elliott Joslin Camp: Boys

Age spread:
Clara Barton Camp: 6–17
Camp Joslin: 7–16½

Per summer:
Clara Barton Camp: 320
Camp Joslin: 350

Campers come from the:
Clara Barton Camp:
Northeast 90% Southeast 2% Central 2%
Northwest 2% Southwest 2% International 2%

Camp Joslin:
Northeast 70% Southeast 11% Central 5%
Northwest 5% Southwest 5% International
4%

Average number of international campers:
Canada 3, Egypt 3, Mexico 3, Spain 3, Bermuda 2, Puerto Rico 2, Virgin Islands 2

Season:
June 25–August 18

Session (by percentage of campers) and cost:
Clara Barton Camp:
2 weeks, 25% (four sessions), $950

Camp Joslin:
2 weeks, 25% (four sessions), $1,000

Extra charges:
None (cost includes all medical/diabetes supplies)

Scholarships:
Clara Barton Camp: 50% of campers do not pay full tuition

Camp Joslin: 55% of campers do not pay full tuition

Financial structure:
Private, not for profit

Founded:
Clara Barton Camp: 1932
Camp Joslin: 1948

Managing Director(s) and years associated with camp:
Clara Barton Camp:
Shelley D. Yeager, 9

Elliott Joslin Camp:
Paul B. Madden, 33

Other Director(s) and years associated with camp:
Clara Barton Camp:
Maria Lang, 13
Kassie Gregono, 7
Joan Mansfield, 3

Elliott Joslin Camp:
Robert Gannon, 22
Richard Keller, M.D., 7

Directors' backgrounds:
Shelley D. Yeager: master's degree in social work; 12 years medical social work; eight years camping experience

Joan Mansfield: M.D., pediatrician

Kassie Gregono: B.A.

Maria Lang: master's degree in education—special needs

Robert Gannon: B.A., education

Richard Keller: M.D., pediatrician

Counselors:
Clara Barton Camp: 20
Women 100% Min. age 18
Ratio to Campers 1: 3

Camp Joslin: 26
Men 100% Min. age 18
Ratio to Campers 1: 3

Health and safety:
Clara Barton Camp:
Infirmary; 4 RNs, physician, and dietitian on staff; hospital nearby; camp supervised by the Joslin Diabetes Center

Camp Joslin:
Infirmary; 2 RNs, 5 physicians and nutritionist on staff; hospital 15 miles away; camp supervised by the Joslin Diabetes Center

Concentration:
Recreation; outdoor challenges; general
sports, hiking, swimming, boating; mastery
of diabetes management

Mission:
"To enable campers to gain knowledge of diabetes management; to instill self-confidence and independence. To allow children with diabetes to be with other children sharing the same challenges. To learn new recreational skills. To promote family acceptance and participation in diabetes care. To help children realize that diabetes is not a limitation, and that they can be all they want to be."

Obviously, these brother and sister camps for children with diabetes are not for all youngsters, but I have included them because, diabetes aside, they represent everything that a fine all-around summer camp should be.

Located a few miles apart in central Massachusetts and supervised by the world-renowned Joslin Diabetes Center in Boston, both camps do a superb job fulfilling their mission of helping active young people become confident and successful at whatever they try to do while they learn how to manage their diabetes.

"We want these children to know that they have a responsibility to themselves and to others," explains Joslin manager Paul Madden. "We want them to learn how to meet the challenges that diabetes presents each day, while having fun."

The Clara Barton Camp for Girls is part of a wonderful, caring heritage, located on the birthplace property of Clara Barton, founder of the American Red Cross and one of history's foremost feminists and humanitarians. Founded in 1932, the camp has served as a model for many diabetes camps around the world.

The Elliott Joslin Camp is located on the site of a nineteenth-century lumber camp and, despite its beautiful private pond, several athletic fields, tennis courts, and basketball courts, the campus still feels remote. The camp has recently added a new Cape Cod site to its facilities.

Both camps have a wonderfully diverse group of youngsters from a variety of income levels and ethnic backgrounds, as well as from all over the United States and the world. Although a number of campers have multifaceted physical handicaps and medical needs, these camps, with their top-notch medical staffs, handle them with ease and confidence.

Most counselors at these camps are camp alumni and therefore diabetics themselves. It is important to them that the youngsters in their care learn as much as they can about the disease itself, as well as how diabetes affects them and those around them. Staffers are always on the lookout for "teachable moments." When there is a diabetic episode, they make sure that everybody involved learns from the experience.

To take advantage of a diabetic's natural energy levels, high energy activities such as swimming, soccer, basketball, and tennis are scheduled after meals, when blood sugar levels are high; activities that require less energy are scheduled before meals. Both camps strive to provide lots of physical exercise and activity so that campers will grow into adults who will continue to be active.

Clara Barton Camp offers swimming, soccer, basketball, volleyball, gymnastics, hiking, games, a sports barn, tennis, cycling, lacrosse, arts and crafts, archery, sign language, boating, softball, newspaper, and drama.

Activities at Camp Joslin include sailing, soccer, canoeing, kayaking, lacrosse, campcraft, jogging, basketball, Ping-Pong, pool, tennis, computers, swimming, weight lifting, street hockey, baseball, softball, fishing, archery, wrestling, hiking, ultimate Frisbee, arts and crafts, football, hockey, paddle boats, radio broadcasting, adventure trail and trips, Project Adventure, and new games. At different times during each session, both camps get together for some coed activities, most notably evening dances.

Meals are carefully prepared at both camps according to each camper's individually planned menu, an easily understood system designed so that the camper knows how much of each food is medically appropriate. The dining rooms in both camps are happy, active, and noisy places, and the food is terrific, all the better to demonstrate how manageable these campers' condition can be.

While general principles of diabetes management are taught at these camps, each camper has his or her own tailor-made management program, and both the medical staff and the individual counselors know what it is. A high staff-return rate and active counselor-in-training program at each camp are good evidence that because these adults got so much from their camping experience, they want a chance to pay it back. These are confident institutions that face demanding educational challenges with good cheer and optimism and continued success. And that is precisely what rubs off on their campers.

Clearwater Camp

Address:
7490 Clearwater Road
Minocqua, Wisconsin 54548

Summer phone:
(715) 356-5030 and (800) 236-5030
Fax (715) 356-3124

Winter phone:
(715) 356-5762 and (800) 236-5030
Fax (715) 356-3124

Natural features:
Located on Tomahawk Lake

Nearest large city or town:
Northwest of Rhinelander, between
Hazelhurst and Minocqua, off U.S. Highway 51

Enrollment:
Girls

Age spread:
8–16

Per summer:
175

Campers come from the:
Northeast 6% Southeast 2% Central 85%
Northwest 3% Southwest 4%

Season:
June 21–August 9

Session (by percentage of campers) and cost:
3½ weeks, 78%, $1,775
7 weeks, 22%, $3,300

Extra charges:
Some (extended riding and waterskiing)

Financial structure:
For profit

Founded:
1933

Owner(s) and years associated with camp:
Sunny Moore, 37

Managing Director(s) and years associated with camp:
Sunny Moore, 37

Director's background:
Sunny Moore: B.A., English, Duke University; camp director 20 years.

Counselors: 34
Women 100% Min. age 19
Ratio to campers 1: 3

Health and safety:
RN on staff; clinic and hospital nearby

Concentration:
Sailing, swimming, canoeing, waterskiing, and windsurfing; riding and tennis; nature studies, trips, camping, arts and crafts

Mission:

"Character, caring, and concern for one another are stressed. Solid teaching of activities gives to campers the opportunity to learn and master new skills at a pace with which they are comfortable, in a loving, non-competitive atmosphere. Activities thus serve as a vehicle for growth rather than an end in themselves."

Clearwater Camp is located on seventy-five acres bordering Tomahawk Lake in north-central Wisconsin. Surrounded by a nature conservancy that protects thousands of acres of natural bogs and marshes, it's a welcoming and orderly wilderness outpost. Paths twist and turn through birches, cedars, and oaks, and signs say things like: "Friends are life's most precious treasures," or "Wilderness invites friendships true."

At the center of Clearwater, overlooking the lake, is a wonderful old lodge that was once a Victorian resort and is now used mainly for worship or rainy day activities. Nineteenth-century books still occupy shelves, and over the mantel of a lovely stone fireplace is yet another sign. It says, "Here let the fires of friendship burn." Like the lodge, many of Clearwater's buildings were built in the early 1900s and have been carefully maintained to retain their authenticity.

Clearwater girls live in groups of five, with a counselor. The youngest (those who have completed grades 2–4) reside in a unit called the Harbor, consisting of enclosed cabins with bathroom facilities and a fireplace. The girls on the Cape (grades 5–6) and those on the Point (grades 7–10) stay in enclosed or tent-sided cabins with central toilet and shower facilities. The three living units are separated from each other, with the Harbor girls living near the main camp buildings, while the Cape and Point girls stay on a five-acre island that is connected to the mainland by a lovely wooden footbridge.

Clearwater's formal program includes eighteen hours of instruction per week in activities that graduate in difficulty as campers get older. Regular activities include archery, arts and crafts, campcraft, canoeing and canoe trips, drama, nature lore, pioneer camping, photography, English riding, sailing, swimming, tennis, tumbling, waterskiing, and windsurfing. Each week the staff prepares a new schedule of activities for each camper, based upon her preferences, her parents' preferences, and the best use of the staff and facilities.

Three times a week, large blocks of time—say, an entire morning or afternoon—are set aside for pursuing nonscheduled individual interests or maybe spending extra time perfecting skills in one of the scheduled activities. An hour every morning and a half hour in the afternoon are free time.

Clearwater makes good use of both its excellent waterfront and wilderness location. The camp's sailing program consists of ten boats, and the goal is clear: Each camper strives to achieve a level where she can skipper a boat in a camp regatta.

The nature program underlies much of camp life and comes into play on the many excursions out of camp. Trips by canoe may go out for two or three days along one of Wisconsin's many northern waterways. Other trips may take campers to a place called the New Land, one of Clearwater's permanent (and quite primitive) sites off in the forest by a trout stream. Trips seldom involve more than eight campers and a counselor. For older, skilled campers there are backpacking and canoe trips of up to ten days that frequently venture into the Canadian wilds.

The dining hall is a wonderful old building, and dining procedures haven't changed since the camp's founding. Girls still sing traditional mealtime songs, are seated according to a seating chart, and observe proper manners throughout. The camp motto, inscribed on the wall in old English lettering, proclaims: "Clearwater is a place for new beginnings." And that it is. Both director and staff work hard to create a comfortable and nurturing environment that feels safe, both physically and psychologically. "At Clearwater," says director Sunny Moore, "nobody is ever left out."

This is a wonderful, traditional camp where people have been doing the same kinds of things for a long time: helping girls and young women build character and have fun. There is a strong sense of integrity here, the kind of institutional self-confidence that comes naturally to a camp with Clearwater's continuity of leadership and experience with young women.

Deerhorn

Summer address:
3725 Deerhorn Road
Rhinelander, Wisconsin 54501

Phone:
(715) 369-0562
Fax (715) 369-9012

Winter address:
3725 Deerhorn Road
Rhinelander, WI 54501 or
1168 Asbury Ave
Winnetka, IL 60093

Phone:
(715) 369-0665 or
(708) 446-6080

Natural features:
Secluded setting on North Pelican Lake, 2
miles from nearest highway; surrounded by
woods

Nearest large city or town:
Rhinelander, northern Wisconsin

Enrollment:
Boys

Age spread:
7–16

Per summer:
300 (150 per session)

Campers come from the:
Northeast 1% Southeast 1% Central 84%
Southwest 2% International 12%

Average number of international campers:
Mexico 24, France 3, Spain 3, Japan 2

Season:
June 19–August 20

Session (by percentage of campers) and cost:
2 weeks, 26%, $950
3 weeks, 28%, $1,350
4 weeks, 29%, $1,800
6 weeks, 11%, $2,290
7 weeks, 4%, $2,760
9 weeks, 2%, $3,140

Extra charges:
Some (ice hockey, riding, certain trips)

Scholarships:
1% of campers do not pay full tuition

Financial structure:
For profit

Founded:
1930

Owner(s) and years associated with camp:
Broadbridge family, 65

Managing Director(s) and years associated with camp:
Don Broadbridge, Jr., 60
Don Broadbridge, III, 37
Blaine Broadbridge, 33
Susan Broadbridge, 14

Directors' backgrounds:
Don Broadbridge, Jr.: graduate, Colgate
University; 35 years director of Deerhorn

Don Broadbridge III: graduate, Duke University; Associate Director since 1981

Blaine Broadbridge: graduate, Kansas University; 8 years school teacher; 15 years Deerhorn staff member and Associate Director

Susan Broadbridge: Associate Director since 1981

Counselors: 30
Men 95% Women 5% Min. age 19
Ratio to campers 1: 5

Health and safety:
Infirmary, RN on staff; most counselors receive First Aid and CPR training during orientation

Concentration:
An impressive variety of activities, with emphasis on athletics and individual "lifetime" sports such as waterskiing, golf, tennis, riding, riflery, etc.

Mission:
From the camp creed: ". . . To play every game on the level, win modestly, lose gracefully, and have a kind word for the opposing side . . . To speak the truth and to think the truth . . . To try to see the other fellow's side of the question and strive for harmony . . . To be kind, because manliness requires kindness . . . To be strong, because self-reliance is born of strength . . . To be a gentleman under all conditions and circumstances."

Deerhorn is at once spacious and isolated, tucked away in the north woods on the shores of a sandy-bottom lake noted for its muskellunge population. It's an ideal spot for outdoor sports, and this camp serves up a variety that is virtually unparalleled in American camping.

The campus is heavily forested, interspersed with rustic cabins and green lawns. The 110-foot-long main lodge, built in the 1930s of Norway spruce logs, could have been designed as a Hollywood set; it is that well preserved. The building houses the main indoor recreation area and two spacious dining rooms. Other camp buildings are similarly built, from logs harvested from the surrounding forest, and equally well maintained.

Deerhorn has remained a family operation since its 1930 founding, by Dr. and Mrs. Don Broadbridge. In 1958 the doctor passed it on to Don, Jr., who in turn handed it over to third generation sons and family. In the sixty-five years of Deerhorn's existence, though educational techniques have evolved, the original values of this camp have not changed one bit, set forth in a camp creed penned by the founder and reprinted on the inside cover of the camp catalog.

The importance of family, and the ways families work, are recurring themes at Deerhorn. Prior to the start of the camping season, the staff hosts a week-long father/son camp. During the regular season, activities are structured so that campers act like brothers—i.e., older boys teaching younger ones, etc. Furthering its commitment to family, all boys are required to write home twice a week.

Deerhorn offers more sessions of differing lengths than most camps. With some sessions overlapping and some boys staying at camp while other groups come and go, parents might be concerned that their son would get bored repeating the same material. At some camps that would indeed be a problem; at Deerhorn there is such a variety of activities that even a nine-weeker can constantly find something new. Baseball, tennis, golf, riflery, crafts, archery, mountain biking, horseback riding, fishing, tripping, basketball, waterskiing, sailing, canoeing, swimming, diving, float boat, music, volleyball, and soccer are just some of the activities offered. A week-long ice hockey program (two hours per day) is offered to boys enrolled in the first three-week or the seven-week session.

Deerhorn enjoys a terrific sailing program, bolstered by a fleet of X-boats, Lightnings, Sunfish, Sailfish, and a Hobie 16 catamaran. Utilizing an impressive waterfront of four docks and a sandy beach that goes out 150 feet before boys reach their depth, swimming here is not only educational but a daily pleasure.

The camp maintains its own stable of horses and teaches boys to saddle, bridle, and groom. Western riding is the specialty here, on several miles of impressive trails. As in all other activities, safety is a big part of the riding program (boys are required to wear helmets while riding).

Competition is not shunned at Deerhorn. Tournaments within camp and with other camps are features of many of the athletics. But winning is not stressed. Boys are awarded "stairs" for their individual progress.

The most coveted prize is the "Leader" award, which has more to do with a young man's attitude than his athletic performance. Each year only four boys are made Leaders, a significant honor considering that nearly all of the counselors here are former Deerhorn Leaders.

The camp creed, written 65 years ago, begins: "To enjoy the Great Outdoors as one of the gifts of life." It only takes a couple of minutes here to begin to understand what Dr. Broadbridge had in mind. Surrounded by majestic pines and a beautiful lake, you hear birds singing and water lapping the shore, while camp dogs laze around in the sun. This is a beautiful and energetic camp with an ambitious program loaded with activities. Everything they do here they do well, with great facilities, great equipment, and superb instruction. It's a place that thrives on the love of family, appreciation of self, and pride of accomplishment; a place where a boy will return summer after summer because he can see, by example of those before him, the kind of young man he wants to be.

Douglas Ranch Camps

Summer address:
33200 East Carmel Valley Road
Carmel Valley, California 93924

Phone:
(408) 659-2761
Fax (408) 659-5690

Winter address:
8 Pala Avenue
Piedmont, CA 94611

Phone:
(510) 547-3925
Fax (510) 653-5036

Natural features:
120 acres of oaks; creek running through
property; 15 miles from Pacific Ocean

Nearest large city or town:
Carmel, Monterey

Enrollment:
Separate but equal programs for boys and
girls

Age spread:
7–15

Per summer:
260

Campers come from the:
Northeast 2% Southeast 2% Central 2%
Northwest 42% Southwest 42% International
10%

**Average number of international
campers:**
26—Japan 9, Mexico 7, England 2, France
2, Germany 2, Hong Kong 2

Season:
June 24–August 27

**Session (by percentage of campers)
and cost:**
2 weeks, 20%, $1,450
3 weeks, 40%, $2,100
4 weeks, 40%, $2,550

Extra charges:
Some (health insurance, laundry, camp store;
average $15–20/week)

Financial structure:
For profit

Founded:
1925 (girls' camp)
1929 (boys' camp)

**Owner(s) and years associated with
camp:**
Ehrhardt family, 70

**Managing Director(s) and years asso-
ciated with camp:**
Carole Douglas Ehrhardt, 40

**Other Director(s) and years associated
with camp:**
Franklin M. Ehrhardt, 29

Directors' backgrounds:
Carole Douglas Ehrhardt: B.A., University
of California, Berkeley; camper, counselor,
program director, assistant director, director
at Douglas

Franklin M. Ehrhardt: B.A., University of California, Berkeley; master's degree, city planning, U.C. Berkeley; camper, counselor, Boy Scouts of America and Douglas Ranch

Counselors: 24
Men 40% Women 60% Min. age 19
Ratio to campers 1: 4

Health and safety:
Infirmary, RN on staff; hospital nearby

Concentration:
Structured (nonelective) program consisting of western riding, swimming, tennis, archery, and riflery

Mission:
"Our main emphasis is to help our campers become well-rounded, happy and productive citizens."

This is a place full of fun and learning, where the emphasis is placed squarely on good manners, sportsmanship, and concern for one another. Even though there are no uniforms, you get the feeling as you walk around the lovely campus that you've wandered into an America of the past. Surrounded by giant oak trees dripping with Spanish moss, everywhere you look you see a magnificent view of the Carmel Valley, while the air sings with strains of old-time camp songs or maybe a sudden distant cheer. Even the camp's general information policy for parents has the feel of a bygone era. "If parents wish to send fruit, candy or other treats," the brochure elucidates, "please send enough for the whole camp."

Despite the rustic feel of the place, all of Douglas Ranch's facilities are in excellent shape. Central to the camp is the lodge, which has three large dining rooms and is used for evening activities such as sing-alongs, skits, and meetings. Also in the center of the camp are four tennis courts, while a short walk brings you to the camp's playing field, a wide, fenced-in area for soccer, baseball, cricket, or whatever else might be scheduled. Below all this is a lovely open-air theater; above, the crafts and newspaper building. Additionally, Douglas Ranch has two archery ranges and a rifle range, a barn and riding ring for its twenty-two horses, and areas for volleyball, paddle tennis, shuffleboard, Ping-Pong, basketball, and tetherball. Most impressive is the seventy-five-foot-long, oval-shaped swimming pool. Ranging from three to nine feet deep, the pool is surrounded by lawns, changing rooms, and bathroom facilities.

Although Douglas Ranch is technically a coed camp, boys and girls have separate activity programs and live in separate areas of the 120-acre campus. Each area has ten cabins (sleeping four to six, plus a counselor) and a central washroom with basins, showers, and toilets. Cabins are rustic, yet clean and well placed.

Sports are central to Douglas Ranch life, built around carefully regulated competition. Soon after arriving, campers are placed on either the Green or Buff team and then spend their days both competing against and cooperating with members of the opposite team, learning that doing things for and *with* others is often the best reward. The program is managed so that all campers can succeed while they learn.

"Our program is a structured one, with children participating in all classes we offer," director Carole Ehrhardt explains. "We want them to have fun at camp, but at the same time they should be learning new skills and acquiring a sense of achievement and greater self-confidence."

Counselors come to Douglas Ranch Camps from several foreign countries and many different states. Prior to the season, the entire staff attends an intensive week-long orientation, with first aid/CPR instruction and familiarization with camp practices.

Even though boys and girls are separated most of the time, they seem to enjoy a casual relationship as paths cross during the day. Evening programs bring the two groups together for events such as folk dances, treasure hunts, skits, carnival nights, campfire sing-alongs, and other events. The campers hold a joint community service every Sunday morning, while Sunday afternoons are generally relaxed times for tennis, swimming, and other activities.

Two lovely dining rooms—one for boys and one for girls—provide family-style settings for sumptuous, healthy meals. Attention is given to table manners, and campers are expected, out of courtesy, to try a small portion of everything offered.

Over the central fireplace in each dining room is an old Grantland Rice quotation that was carved in wood in the early 1920s. It says: "When the One Great Scorer comes to write against your name, He marks not that you won or lost, but how you played the game." Here at Douglas, that is what they are all about.

Camp Dudley YMCA

Address:
Westport, NY 12993

Phone:
(518) 962-4720

Natural features:
Situated on Lake Champlain

Nearest large city or town:
Port Henry, NY; across the lake from Burlington, VT

Enrollment:
Boys

Age spread:
$10^1/_2$–15

Per summer:
540

Campers come from the:
Northeast 81% Southeast 5% Central 5% Northwest 1% Southwest 3% International 5%

Season:
Late June to late August

Session (by percentage of campers) and cost:
4 weeks, 70%, $1,850
8 weeks, 30%, $3,375

Extra charges:
None

Scholarships:
20% of campers do not pay full tuition

Financial structure:
YMCA, not for profit

Founded:
1885

Owner(s) and years associated with camp:
Camp Dudley, Inc., 84

Managing Director(s) and years associated with camp:
William J. Schmidt, Ph.D., 49

Director's background:
William J. Schmidt: M.A. and Ph.D., American history, University of North Carolina; physical therapist; school teacher; camp director for 20 years

Head Counselors: 40
Men 100% Min. age 18, average age 23
Ratio to campers 1: 7

Health and safety:
Infirmary, 2 RNs on staff; MD on call

Concentration:
Athletics, drama, hiking and trips, art, chorus

Mission:

"We are interested in the spiritual and physical development of a youngster. We are interested in his character, leadership skills and spiritual growth. The camp's motto is 'the other fellow first.'"

Camp Dudley is a gorgeous, first-rate camp on the shores of Lake Champlain, in Adirondack farm country. The main campus has 250 acres and more than two miles of lake frontage, with other land (and a reservoir) used as a hiking outpost in the Adirondack foothills.

Facilities are tremendous, both in scope and in the quality of maintenance. There are four baseball diamonds, six basketball courts (2 indoor), four soccer fields, a lacrosse field, eight tennis courts, archery and rifle ranges, an all-weather 200-meter track, and a swimming and diving area with a racing pool. I want to stress how immaculately all of these facilities are kept, particularly the tennis and basketball courts and the gym, a wonderful building that is wanting for nothing. Dudley also has a superb theater to house its equally superb drama program.

Campers are organized into four divisions: Cubs (10–11½), Plebes (11½–12½), Juniors (12½–13½), and Seniors (13½–15). Their thirty-eight cabins line the shore and the perimeter of the main campus. The virtues of cleanliness are not taken lightly here. Every day after breakfast and again after rest period campers are expected to put their cabins in order.

Activities at Dudley include archery, diving, basketball, fishing, flag football, photography, publications, dramatics, skin diving, softball, golf, lacrosse, lifesaving, music training in both instruments and voice, volleyball, water basketball, weight lifting, boating, canoeing, arts and crafts, and a fine tripping program, with three- to five-day canoe trips or hikes into the Adirondacks for older boys and shorter canoeing or hiking overnights for all.

Dudley maintains a keen intramural program in athletics such as tennis, wrestling, baseball, soccer, track, swimming, riflery, and sailing. Every boy is assigned to at least one team, and there are plenty of pickup games and opportunities to sign up for instruction in all the sports, as well as in art, music, or dramatics. Underlying values are fair play, generosity to your opponent, and good conduct and language.

Special activities throughout the summer include aquatic meets, sailing regattas, treasure hunts, musicals, mass sings, glee clubs, orchestras, Saturday night shows, and dramatics. There are several glee clubs, a big band, and a concert band. Anybody who plays an instrument is encouraged to bring it along. And writers will want to join the staff of the camp publications.

Meals at Dudley are on an all-you-can-eat (but eat-all-you-take) basis. The dining room is attractive and clean, the kitchen top-notch, and every camper takes his turn waiting on tables, about once a week.

Dudley campers gather every morning for a chapel talk, and every evening they meet for vespers. On Sundays everyone gathers at the outdoor chapel for Sunday service, often featuring guest speakers, and on Sunday evening the camp comes together for a mass hymn-sing followed by a concert of hymns played by the brass ensemble.

Even though there is a lot of competition here, probably the most competitive feature of Camp Dudley is its admissions. The camp is usually full by February, due to both the high rate of returning campers and the camp's well-deserved reputation. Camp Dudley sets a standard for alumni loyalty; former campers not only help fund and manage the camp, but they return for alumni gatherings at the end of every season and meet at some of the forty-five reunions held every year in cities across the country.

This camp aims to develop values and leadership qualities in its campers, and that is exactly what it does. There are several awards: Emblems for the Cubs and Plebes, a Bronze Button for Juniors, and the Camp Flag for Seniors. The Camp Emblem means that a camper has practiced "the other fellow first" and has gained the respect and approval of his fellow campers and leaders. Emphasis is placed on a camper's working for the good of his cabin group.

This is one of those rare places where good, caring people are brought together as if by magic. It's the kind of thing that comes along every now and then that you figure just can't last. But people here tell me that this spirit has been here as long as they can remember. The place simply exudes hugging and compassion as it brings out the best qualities in all of its people.

Perhaps what makes the atmosphere so magical is its dynamic leader, William Schmidt. As you walk around and meet people, it becomes obvious how much the others—staff and campers alike—emulate this man. His spiritual values are an integral part of the camp, whose heart is always in its motto: "The other fellow first."

Elk Creek Ranch and Trek Program

ELK CREEK RANCH

Summer address:
P.O. Box 1476
Cody, Wyoming 82414

Phone:
(307) 587-3902

Winter address:
31A Academy Street
South Berwick, ME 03908

Phone:
(207) 384-5361

Natural features:
160 acres located in a 6,000-foot valley; surrounded by two mountain ranges and the Shoshone National Forest; a trout creek runs through the campus

Nearest large city or town:
Look for Cody, in northwestern corner of Wyoming

Enrollment:
Coed
Boys 50% Girls 50%

Age spread:
13–17

Per summer:
60 (30 per session)

Campers come from the:
Northeast 90% Southeast 2% Central 2% Northwest 2% Southwest 2% International 2%

Average number of international campers:
France 5

Season:
June 20–August 18

Session (by percentage of campers) and cost:
4 weeks, 95%, $2,350
8 weeks, 5%, $3,500

Extra charges:
Some (optional Yellowstone and Teton trip: $130; fishing licenses: $10–$40; canteen $75)

Financial structure:
Private, not for profit

Founded:
1957

Owner(s) and years associated with camp:
Ridgway family, 37

Managing Director(s) and years associated with camp:
Susan W. Ridgway, 23

Other Director(s) and years associated with camp:
Tina Moore, 28
Rob Plakke, 5
Debby Moore, 29

Directors' backgrounds:
Susan W. Ridgway: B.A., psychology and art history; private high school coach

Tina Moore: B.A., University of Montana; high school English teacher

Rob Plakke: B.A., University of Montana; outdoorsman; tree farmer

Debby Moore: B.A., art, University of Washington; art teacher

Counselors: 14–16
Men 50% Women 50% Min. age 16
Ratio to Campers 1: 2¹/₂

Health and Safety:
Medical center one hour away

Concentration:
Ranch-work activities and Western riding including trail rides, barrel racing, and pack trips

Mission:
 "To provide a safe, healthy Western wilderness experience. We hope to foster daily goal-setting and accomplishment through our work program. All ranchers are involved with a variety of ranch chores, from building and maintaining fences to halter training our two-month-old horses."

Elk Creek Ranch is a unique camp in that it advertises itself as a place where young people come to work, among other things. But it's the kind of work that is the stuff of romance to many people nowadays—training horses, mending fences, building a bunkhouse. This is a working Western ranch, and its location is the most remote of any of the camps mentioned in this book—the gravel entrance to the camp is a hair-raising twenty-eight miles long, over a mountain—but it's also one of the most beautiful. Here you're surrounded by snowcapped peaks and serenaded continually by a wide trout brook that winds through the middle of camp. Elk Creek Ranch is also the smallest camp I've visited. Enrollment is limited to thirty campers (fifteen boys and fifteen girls) for each of its two sessions, making it feel and behave like a close-knit family.

Indeed, there is a great deal of family commitment here. Elk Creek started as a family vacation spot and turned into a teenage camping program in 1957. The current owners are second generation, and they are gradually turning the reins over to their own children. This is a casual place run by people who love the hard, satisfying life of the rugged West and the pleasure of shared experiences in a matchless setting. They talk with equal facility about hard rides and good books, and they enjoy both.

Elk Creek is not heavily programmed. Instead, it's a camp where teenagers are supervised yet can freely choose for themselves how to spend their free time. It's a place where, whatever they choose, there will be lots of physical demands. Goals are clear, and so are the rewards.

Elk Creek offers two different programs, which can be taken separately or in combination with one another: the Ranch Program, which features horseback riding and ranch work; and the Trek Program, which concentrates on extensive wilderness backpacking.

All ranchers are given their own horses and riding gear for the duration of their stay, and they are responsible for feeding, grooming, and saddling their mounts. In addition, the ranchers spend two hours a day, four or five days a week, on chores that include mending and building fences, repairing corrals, irrigating pastures, and feeding horses.

Within the Ranch Program are two separate programs: the Riding Program and the Work Program. As their names suggest, those in the riding program concentrate on horses, going on trail rides that cover a hundred square miles, and developing advanced riding skills. At the end of the session, the camp offers a gymkhana (games on horseback) and a four-day pack trip. Those in the Work Program concentrate more on ranch chores (older campers are eligible for small tuition refunds depending on the amount of time they put in), tackling at least one extensive building project and also taking responsibility for training the camp's horses.

Of course, the Ranch Program is not all ranch work and horses. There are lots of other options. Skiers can go glacier skiing at 10,000 feet in the Beartooth Mountains; anglers can go fishing in rivers and lakes; and trippers can go on three-day car caravans through Yellowstone and Teton national parks (including, optionally, mountain climbing school and the Grand Teton climb). Rifle- and trap-shooting and backpacking are also available. At the end of each Ranch session, Ranchers go on a four-day trip into one of the most remote areas of Sunlight County.

The Trek Program offers two trips of extended duration. The Absaroka Trek concentrates on mountain travel and ascents, and concludes with a six-day trip to the Tetons. There, Trekkers are introduced to the basics of technical rock climbing for two days, after which they climb one of the high peaks of the Tetons. The Beartooth Trek is an extended hike across a high plateau populated by thousands of pristine lakes.

The counselors here are carefully hand-picked from previous groups of Elk Creek Ranchers and Trekkers. Most Junior Counselors have spent at least two years on the ranch as nonsalaried C.I.T.s (counselors-in-training) prior to being counselors.

All buildings on the ranch are log structures. Some date back to the turn of the century, when pioneering homesteaders set down roots here. Today's ranchers stay in log cabin bunkhouses that are equipped with electricity and hot and cold running water. And every bunkhouse has several fly rods leaning against the wall, ready to do battle. The grub is plentiful and very tasty, as you'd expect after a hard day of riding, mending fences, or just fishing, and the dining room is always welcoming, cozy, and full of good, solid friends.

Farm & Wilderness Camps

(NOTE: comprising five distinct residential camps)

Address:
HCR 70, Box 27
Plymouth, Vermont 05056

Phone:
(802) 422-3761

Natural features:
3,000 acres of lakes, streams, and forest in the Green Mountains

Nearest large city or town:
Rutland

Enrollment:
Coed
Boys 50% Girls 50%

Age spread:
9–14

Per summer:
320

Campers come from the:
Northeast 80% Southeast 13% Central 5%
Northwest 1% Southwest 1%

Season:
June 25–August 17

Session (by percentage of campers) and cost:
4 weeks, 40%, $2,250
8 weeks, 60%, $3,600

Extra charges:
None

Scholarships:
12% of campers do not pay full tuition

Financial structure:
Private, not for profit

Founded:
1939

Owner(s) and years associated with camp:
Farm & Wilderness, 21

Managing Director(s) and years associated with camp:
Leonard K. Cadwallader, 19

Other Director(s) and years associated with camp:
David Martin, 22
Rebecca Steinitz, 5

Directors' backgrounds:
Leonard K. Cadwallader: B.A., Earlham College; business owner before coming to Farm & Wilderness

David Martin: B.A., Williams College; M.B.A., Harvard

Rebecca Steinitz: B.A., Yale University; Ph.D., University of California, Berkeley

Counselors: 80
Men 50% Women 50% Min. age 19
Ratio to campers 1: 3

Health and safety:
4 RNs on staff; physician on call; health center 18 miles away

Concentration:
Large group projects

Mission:
"It is difficult for a child to feel confident and bold when faced with the complexities of life today . . . The essence of Farm & Wilderness can be found in the Quaker values of simplicity, honesty, self-reliance and respect for all persons."

If you never thought work could be fun, you'll be in for the surprise of your life at this camp. Here camp chores are put in their most positive light: as a way of accomplishing a common goal through positive—make that *enjoyable*—participation in a group. The camp's motto, forged by its founders, Ken and Susan Webb, is "Work is love made visible."

Farm & Wilderness Camps are located on 650 acres on a mile-long lake at the foot of Vermont's second-highest mountain. Most of the land abuts Vermont State Forest, giving campers thousands of acres and many miles of trails to explore. At the heart of this place are the values associated with Quaker and modern homesteading ethics: close community life, cooperation, and the sharing of work and fun.

The minute you walk into this camp, you know you're in a place that's a little different. Instead of a soccer game, you hear the sound of hammers going hard, cocks crowing, and sheep bleating. You hear singing, you see youngsters having the time of their lives—doing hard work. In many ways, this is like stepping back in time, to a nineteenth-century New England farm, or maybe a seventeenth-century Native American village.

Farm & Wilderness Camps are actually five different residential camps (and a family camp and day camp, too), some single sex and some coed. Flying Cloud is a primitive camp for 40 boys between the ages of 11 and 14. Here campers live in tepees, wear breechcloths, and learn to live like Native Americans, using the skills of the woods. Indian Brook is for 125 girls, from 9 through 14, and is patterned after nineteenth-century New England farm life, with the addition of certain camp activities such as a waterfront program, singing, dancing, and campcraft. Timberlake, for 125 boys aged 9 through 14, is Indian Brook's counterpart. Boys do building, farm work, and lots of swimming, sailing, hiking, and all-around playing. Tamarack Farm, for 72 boys and girls, ages 15–17, might be seen as the next step in the younger boys' and girls' experiences in rustic farm camp settings. As you would expect from a camp that celebrates the modern homesteading ethic, there is no difference in the programs offered to girls and boys. Saltash Mountain, for 40 boys and girls, ages 11–14, is a hiking camp, but with plenty of in-camp activities, too. Families interested in any of these camps should see the camp brochure for details of the camp most appropriate for their favorite camper.

Since the founding of Farm & Wilderness Camps in 1939, campers and staff have built—with hand tools and group muscle power—all of the camps' facilities, from the open, three-sided cabins spread along the lake shore, to the barn and stables, to the lovely main lodge with its stone fireplace and massive supports. A dedication inside the lodge reads: "We gather here for Ken and Susan. A building built. Love made visible."

As director Leonard Cadwallader explains, "When children realize that they are collectively stronger than what they can be individually, then each child, no matter how insecure, has a chance to shine because the pressure of individual success has been released."

A good example of the Quaker concern for simplicity is that Farm & Wilderness keeps a horse and buggy (which delivers the mail) as a visual reminder that there is another way to live other than by dependence on internal combustion engines and power tools. On the back of the buggy is a sign that says, "Grass power, not gas power."

Community service projects—some environmental and some social (such as aiding a local battered women agency)—is another way these youngsters learn about compassion, justice, and community responsibility. The garden and farm animals provide a continual lesson on how we humans fit into the food chain.

At Farm & Wilderness, kids learn that they share ownership of their camp and its program. They live in cabins built by predecessors, and they build cabins for their successors. They eat food that they grow, and they have important input in the design of their activities. Here youngsters learn to take hold of their own destinies, to value themselves as individuals, and to give equal value to the people around them.

"We aim to give back to each child the natural confidence with which he or she was born," explains Cadwallader. "By providing a very primitive setting where real challenges can be met and mastered, a child can begin to believe in his or her own ability to not only survive, but to succeed."

Gold Arrow Camp

Summer address:
P.O. Box 155, Highway 168
Lakeshore, California 93634

Phone:
(209) 893-6641 or (800) 554-2267

Winter address:
P.O. Box 3755
Santa Monica, CA 90408

Phone:
(800) 554-2267

Natural features:
Located on Huntington Lake in the Sierra
National Forest, elevation 7,000 feet

Nearest large city or town:
Fresno is 65 miles southwest

Enrollment:
Coed
Boys 57% Girls 43%

Age spread:
6–16

Per summer:
900

Campers come from the:
Northeast 4% Southeast 4% Central 4%
Northwest 8% Southwest 68% International
12%

**Average number of international
campers:**
Mexico 35, Japan 10, France 7, Britain 3,
China 3, Germany 3, Indonesia 3, Korea 3,
Saudi Arabia 3

Season:
June 26–August 27

On Huntington Lake in the High Sierra
Established 1933

**Session (by percentage of campers)
and cost:**
1 week, 10%, $725
2 weeks, 40%, $1,450
3 weeks, 25%, $1,850
4 weeks, 25%, $2,500

Extra charges:
Very little (camp store and yearbook, both
optional)

Financial structure:
For profit

Founded:
1933

**Owner(s)/Directors and years associ-
ated with camp:**
Audrey Kremer Monke, 10
Steve Monke, 6

Director's background:
Audrey Kremer Monke: graduate, Stanford
University; 6th grade teacher; member
WAIC Board of Directors; certified camp
director; member, ACA Board of Directors

Counselors: 75
Men 60% Women 40% Min. age 19
Ratio to campers 1: 4

Health and safety:
2 RNs on staff, all staff first aid and CPR
certified

Concentration:
Waterfront; wilderness backpacking; ropes
courses—individual achievement sports

Mission:
"Our program is designed to develop self-confidence through accomplishment in a non-competitive atmosphere. Each camper receives individual attention and participates in all activities."

Gold Arrow Camp looks down from 7,000 feet of elevation in California's High Sierras. Its twenty-seven acres border a six-mile-long lake, providing for a water sports program that is one of the best I've seen anywhere. And the camp is situated inside U.S. Forest Service wilderness lands, giving the Forest Service jurisdiction over not only how the land is used, but what kinds of structures can be erected there.

Consequently, the facilities at Gold Arrow are functional and very well maintained, but never extravagant. The environment remains natural, wild, and preserved, the campus sharing land with majestic ponderosa pines. Campers live in large canvas tents on wooden platforms, and they sleep in sleeping bags on mattress-covered army cots. Up here in the mountains, the summer climate is nearly perfect. Daytime temperatures range from the high 70s to the low 80s, while nights drop to the 50s. Rainfall is zero to less than a half inch, and pollen is almost nonexistent.

Gold Arrow manages to juggle a schedule that is accommodating to its campers but somewhat complicated to implement. There are eight separate sessions, from one to four weeks in duration. The one-week session is a "specialty camp," in which campers advance their skills in one area of the program: either backpacking, horseback riding, sailing, or waterskiing. In the other sessions campers participate in all activities (exception: two-weekers don't go on a backpacking trip), including overnight trips to the camp's Shaver Lake waterskiing outpost. Such scheduling is a feat of stellar management, and the people at Gold Arrow handle it with ease.

Cabin solidarity is the key. Same-session campers are placed in cabins by age and school grade (friends may be placed together as long as they make the request on the application and they are within a year of the same age). Cabin groups eat together, participate in activities together, and go on overnights together.

The aim of Gold Arrow Camp is to develop its youngsters' interests and skills in outdoor sports within a program that encourages the development of self-confidence through non-competitive accomplishment. The sports offered here are those in which people can participate throughout their lives. Emphasis is on participation and learning, and, naturally, having fun—but never on beating an opponent.

The activities program is roughly grouped into two areas: waterfront and wilderness activities. Among the waterfront offerings, the sailing program is particularly praiseworthy. The camp owns 60 national class sailboats, including catamarans, sloops, Sunfish, Super Sunfish, Minifish, Zumas, and Flippers. The entire fleet is put to its best use, allowing all sailors, from beginning through advanced, to improve their skills at their own speeds, while still enjoying the process. Other water sports include windsurfing, waterskiing, jet skiing, hydrosliding, canoeing, kayaking, and motorboating.

The backpacking program utilizes Gold Arrow's outstanding natural surroundings. Trips into the High Sierras range from overnight to four days. Other activities include horseback riding, rock climbing, arts and crafts, archery, riflery, campfires and skits, and a fine ropes course.

Older campers may apply for the Campers in Leadership Training Program. These C.I.T.s, besides participating in other activities, assist counselors or instructors in areas of interest, and they take workshops aimed at improving leadership, interpersonal skills, and self-esteem.

The camp's big covered dining porch is a real treat and so is the food. The menu offers many options, quantities are unlimited, there's a bakery for special desserts, and a fresh salad bar is served at both lunch and dinner. And to enhance the atmosphere, birds fly in and out as you eat.

Gold Arrow is a top-notch camp, sometimes polished, sometimes gritty, but always with its eye on the mission: promoting a solid reverence for self, surroundings, and others.

Hidden Valley Camp

Address:
Freedom, Maine 04941

Phone:
(207) 342-5177 or (800) 922-6737

Natural features:
Located 5 miles from seacoast on 300 acres of fields and forest, with a private lake

Nearest large city or town:
Waterville, Belfast

Enrollment:
Coed
Boys 45% Girls 55%

Age spread:
8–13

Per summer:
405

Campers come from the:
Northeast 75% Southeast 10% Central 10% International 5%

Average number of international campers:
26—France 5, Russia 4, Venezuela 4, Israel 3, Japan 3, Brazil 2, Germany 2

Season:
June 25–August 18

Session (by percentage of campers) and Cost:
4 weeks, 80%, $2,495
8 weeks, 20%, $4,150

Extra charges:
Some (horseback riding, etc.)

Financial structure:
For profit

Founded:
1945

Owner(s) and years associated with camp:
Peter and Meg Kassen, 15

Managing Director(s) and years associated with camp:
Peter and Meg Kassen, 15

Directors' backgrounds:
Peter Kassen: M.B.A., Yale University, specializing in group dynamics and small organizations; B.A. psychology/anthropology, Oberlin College; 15 years camp administration; professional counselor

Meg Kassen: B.S., Philadelphia College of Textiles and Science; 10 years camp administration; teacher

Counselors: 66
Men 45% Women 55% Min. age 20
Ratio to campers 1: 3$^1/_3$

Health and safety:
Infirmary, 4 RNs on staff; hospital 14 miles away

Concentration:
Creative and performing arts; riding

Mission:
"We know there are plenty of young people who enjoy sports but don't like the pressure of too much competition. So we keep the atmosphere low-key and friendly and make sure that everyone is included. The goal is to do your best, not necessarily to be the best."

Hidden Valley Camp is a coed camp for young children that focuses on creative arts, international understanding, and the love of nature. Located near Maine's mid-coast, the campus's three hundred acres are secluded in a wooded valley with its own mile-long lake, a wide river, and no neighbors for several miles. Upon your arrival, your first impression might be of a farm, with the camp farmhouse, barn, and animal corrals. But several trails will soon lead you into a large and abundantly equipped summer camp filled with happy kids.

This is a camp with as finely defined a philosophy as you'll find and a place that lives, eats, and breathes those beliefs. "We have no rifles, uniforms, or religious services," states one of its brochures. "We cherish the values associated with these terms: *acceptance* regardless of gender, race or background; *freedom* to be who you really are; *responsibility* to one's community and peers; and *creativity* in all dimensions of a child's experience."

About 20 percent of the staff come from countries such as Australia, Holland, Britain, and New Zealand, enhancing Hidden Valley's one-world philosophy. Along with the rest of the counselors, they participate in a rigorous twelve-day orientation prior to the season, certainly one of the most ambitious training sessions of any camp I've seen.

Activity programs are free choice for the campers, 100 percent coed, and include a wide number of opportunities in each of eight general areas: arts and crafts, riding (English style), performing arts, sports, waterfront, ropes course, Indian Village, and llama and animal care. (Yes, llamas. Hidden Valley owns the largest herd of llamas in Maine, along with sheep, rabbits, cows, and other farm animals, which campers feed and care for.)

The riding program concentrates on English riding skills, with a Specialty Riding Group for experienced riders who live with the riding staff and take responsibility for their own horses, feeding, grooming, and tacking-up each day. Special programs include participation in area horse shows, showing and jumping in camp parades and festivals, riding overnights, and late afternoon trail rides.

The camp has a waterfront that is not only a lovely spot for swimming instruction, kayaking, canoeing, windsurfing, synchronized swimming, and fishing but is assuredly one of the few camp waterfronts in America with a lakeside pavilion, sauna, and hot tub.

Most campers at Hidden Valley live in one of seventeen cabins, each with indoor showers and lavatories and up to three counselors. The campers in Indian Village, however, stay in four big tepees on a secluded hillside, where they learn traditional Native American crafts and campcraft skills.

Although Hidden Valley's sports program is decidedly noncompetitive, campers do participate in team sports such as basketball, softball, tennis, floor hockey, ultimate Frisbee, volleyball, and soccer. Other athletics include jogging, hiking, gymnastics, adventure club, and aerobics.

What really sets this camp apart are its programs in performing arts and arts and crafts, both led by professionals in their respective fields. Theater arts take form in improvisation, theater games, mime, clowning, comedy workshops, and two monthly camp shows. All types of dance—modern, ballet, jazz, and tap—are taught by professional dance teachers in a fully equipped dance studio. Gymnastics instruction uses the low balance beam, mini-trampoline, and floor exercises, with performances scheduled every two weeks.

Arts and crafts facilities include four stained-glass shops, where campers create kaleidoscopes, window hangings, lamp shades, mirrors, fused glass sculpture, and jewelry. There's a large pottery studio with both kick and electric wheels and three kilns; a modern, well-equipped darkroom for the camp's photography program; and up-to-date facilities for a plethora of other activities ranging from silkscreening and weaving to fabric design, cartooning, and video filming. The performing arts program is enhanced by a fine multipurpose building, which includes modern stage, lighting and sound systems, and an expansive costume and props room.

There is no junk food at Hidden Valley (and no TV or radios allowed). As you might expect, the food here is always fresh, nutritious, and somewhat international in scope, with desserts that include chocolate mousse, fresh raspberry crisp, homemade carrot cake, etc.

In many ways, Hidden Valley is an easy camp to talk about because it is unique and because it does exactly what it sets out to do, and more, with style and a lot of heart.

A sign in the main office reads: "What is man without the beasts? If all the beasts were gone, men would die from great loneliness of spirit. For whatever happens to the beasts also happens to man. All things are connected. Whatever befalls the earth befalls the sons of the earth.—Chief Seattle, 1854"

Camp Highlands for Boys

Summer address:
8450 Camp Highlands Road
Sayner, Wisconsin 54560
Fax (715) 542-3868

Winter address:
4146 Lawn Avenue
Western Springs, IL 60558

Phone:
(800) 868-3398
Fax (708) 246-3216

Natural features:
Located on Plum Lake, surrounded by
Northern Highlands State Forest

Nearest large city or town:
Eagle River, Minocqua; northwest of
Rhinelander

Enrollment:
Boys

Age spread:
8–16

Per summer:
200

Campers come from the:
Northeast 5% Southeast 5% Central 75%
Northwest 5% Southwest 5% International
5%

Average number of international campers:
Mexico 10, France 5, Germany 2, Japan 2

Season:
June 25–August 12

Session (by percentage of campers) and cost:
2 weeks, 16%, $1,000
3 weeks, 33%, $1,400
4 weeks, 35%, $1,875
7 weeks, 16%, $3,100

Extra charges:
Some (long trips—$85)

Financial structure:
For profit

Founded:
1904

Owner(s) and years associated with camp:
Camp Highlands Board of Directors, 37

Managing Director(s) and years associated with camp:
Michael Bachmann, 45

Director's background:
Michael Bachmann: B.A., Grinnell College;
M.S., Northern Illinois University; former
camper, CIT, counselor, division head, pro-
gram director and director; former teacher
and principal; currently heads Education
Department at College of DuPage; Standards
Chair, ACA (Illinois); President, Midwest
Association of Independent Camps; National
Vice-President of ACA; President, Private-
Independent Camp Council

Counselors: 42
Men 93% Women 7% Min. age 18
Ratio to campers 1: 3

Health and safety:
Infirmary, RN on staff; doctors on call;
hospital 20 miles away

Concentration:
A wide variety of activities that are fairly structured in that boys are assigned to every activity at some time, although there are also optional choice times each day—favorites tend to be waterskiing, sailing, fishing, adventure ropes, and wilderness trips

Mission:
"We seek to take advantage of our wilderness setting as we provide an accepting environment for boys to have fun. The fun we have is rooted in what we call the Best Camper Qualities. These include consideration, clean thoughts and clean speech, good sportsmanship, perseverance, honesty and initiative. Our camp motto is 'I'm third.' In its simplest form, that means we try to keep God first, others second, and ourselves third."

Camp Highlands occupies 2,100 feet of peninsular shoreline on Plum Lake, up in the heart of Wisconsin's premier lakes region. Completely surrounded by state forest, Highlands' entrance—stone pillars with a bronze memorial to its alumni, along with a large welcoming banner—is a solid yet cordial symbol of what this camp is all about.

"It is important to us that the boys become well-rounded," explains the camp brochure. "They should be able to skipper a sailboat as well as they play tennis, windsurf, water-ski, skin-dive, or put up a tent. The staff members who grew up spending summers at camp tend to be able to do almost anything!"

Befitting such a statement, the program sets out to expose these boys to a wealth of instruction through a mix of required and elective activities, including archery, baseball, basketball, canoeing, crafts, drama, fishing, golf, nature, photography, riflery, ropes course, sailing, skin diving, soccer, swimming, tennis, track and field, tripping, volleyball, waterskiing, and windsurfing. Each activity has carefully built-in learning levels so that the program grows more challenging as campers get older.

Highlands' facilities include two swimming areas, twelve sailboats, twelve Windsurfers, two ski boats, twenty-five canoes, eight rowboats, five tennis courts, a running track, a rifle and archery range, soccer and baseball fields, a basketball court, a two-hole golf course, ropes course, crafts shop, and a wonderful set of diving towers.

In addition to its in-camp program, Senior campers (14–16) may choose from three optional trips: canoeing in the Minnesota-Canada boundary waters, backpacking the wilds of Isle Royale National Park, or sailing a thirty-foot yacht among the Apostle Islands of Lake Superior.

Each boy lives in one of twenty-six cabins with four or five other boys and a counselor. Visiting parents and alumni may stay at the Highlands Lodge, which consists of six cabins and its own dining hall, and guests are welcome to use many of the camp's facilities.

The dining hall is a great old building by the lakeside, airy and rustic, and filled with long, clean tables and benches. The food is plentiful and delicious, and the atmosphere is just what an American camper from any time in the twentieth century might expect. On the wall hang a big American flag, a huge mounted fish, and an assortment of canoe paddles from years gone by.

This camp has everything going for it. Founded in 1904, it's a bastion of tradition right down to the camp bugler. Although there are few frills, it's the kind of environment that promises some level of success to every boy who comes here, and the more honest effort he puts into it, the greater his successes will be. The director is a mature educator with worlds of experience, and the staff is comprised of folks who are kind and who see every boy as an individual who matters. In a word, it's a place that works. The campers and staff prove that year after year by returning at a rate of between 80 and 85 percent, a very high number. For boys of all ages, this is not only a place to learn and grow, but a safe haven in which to do so.

Camp High Rocks

Address:
P.O. Box 127-A
Cedar Mountain, North Carolina 28718

Phone:
(704) 885-2153

Natural features:
On 1,100 acres of woodland, with an 11-acre private lake, at an elevation of 3,000 feet

Nearest large city or town:
Brevard; between Greenville and Asheville

Enrollment:
Boys

Age spread:
8–15

Per summer:
360

Campers come from the:
Northeast 2% Southeast 96% Central 2%

Season:
Mid-June to mid-August

Session (by percentage of campers) and cost:
2 weeks, 33%, $1,025
3 weeks, 33%, $1,425
4 weeks, 33%, $1,875

Extra charges:
None

Scholarships:
5% of campers do not pay full tuition

Financial structure:
For profit

Founded:
1958

Camp
High Rocks

Owner(s) and years associated with camp:
Henry and Townsend Birdsong, 8, 33

Managing Director(s) and years associated with camp:
Henry Birdsong, 8
Townsend Birdsong, 33

Directors' backgrounds:
Henry Birdsong: B.A., recreation administration, University of North Carolina; certified Red Cross Water Safety Instructor, CPR instructor, first aid instructor; nine years camp counselor; seven years camp director; course director for Discovery, Inc.; staff member, Outward Bound

Townsend Birdsong: B.A., nursing, University of North Carolina; grew up in High Rocks; counselor, instructor in tennis, canoeing, horseback; camp nurse; four years in hospital emergency units; seven years as camp director

Counselors: 55
Men 67% Women 33% Min. age 19
Ratio to campers 1: 3

Health and safety:
Infirmary, 2 RNs on staff; doctor on call; hospital 8 miles away

Concentration:
Mountaineering, rock climbing, canoeing, horseback riding, hiking

Mission:

"Our mission is to help campers develop self-confidence and independence within a cooperative community. Counselors in each activity teach a progression of skills, offer noncompetitive challenges and lead in safe adventures. We are dedicated to personal growth, teamwork, understanding the natural world, and having fun."

High Rocks is an adventure camp, with objectives and skills similar to those of Outward Bound programs. The campus occupies 1,100 acres of woodland, with an eleven-acre private lake, lots of natural rock climbs, and nine miles of hiking and riding trails. From its long, hickory- and oak-lined entrance to its beautifully manicured campus, High Rocks feels like a remote, rustic estate, and campers and staff alike take pride in keeping it that way.

Cabins are neat and clean and all have their own bathroom and private shower facilities. The cabin group—five or six campers, with a counselor—assumes responsibility for cabin cleanliness and goes on outings and overnight camping trips together. Notable among High Rocks' facilities is a fine gymnasium, which houses a full-size basketball court, a fifty-three-foot climbing tower with 4,000 square feet of artificial rock-climbing surface, a high ropes course, a craft shop, and a fifty-foot indoor rifle range in the basement.

High Rocks offers three sessions: a three-week session for boys 8–14, a four-week session for boys 8–15, and, for boys 8–12, a two-week session designed as an introduction to camping activities.

High Rocks' program is freer than most, allowing each boy to choose his own daily schedule and change that schedule if he wishes, the only stipulation being that he remain active. Certain activities, such as riding lessons, meet at particular times due to scheduling. Otherwise, there is the added flexibility whereby a camper may spend extra time in any of his activities, whether it's completing a crafts project or mastering a knot in rock climbing.

Besides the three major programs in mountaineering, canoeing, and riding, boys may choose from swimming, tennis, sports (soccer, volleyball, kickball, Frisbee, etc.), crafts, gym (basketball, four-square, etc.), sailing, riflery, and archery. Although competition is a part of some activities, it is never used as a motivator, nor is it emphasized in the learning process.

High Rocks' Mountaineering Program offers daily hikes, backpacking trips of up to five days, and rock-climbing trips ranging from thirty-foot climbs on camp property to nearby multi-pitch climbs. Every camper participates in this program to some degree, learning to live safely and comfortably in the wilds. A typical hike may be a cabin overnighter to explore a new area or maybe to identify birds or wildflowers, a "get-lost" hike in which maps and compasses come into play, or a three-day backpacking trip into the wilderness areas of Pisgah National Forest.

The Riding Program offers daily instruction, cross-country, trail riding, and jumping. All riders are assured of riding every day, whether for progress or just for fun. In addition to classes in ring and field, there are relaxing trail rides through the woods, bareback riding, moonlight and lunch rides, riding overnights, treasure hunts on horseback, and gymkhana (games on horseback).

The Canoeing Program offers daily lake instruction and river trips. As boys gain experience, they gradually take on more challenging rivers. Trips are frequent, with a group departing nearly every day. Besides canoeing, there are many other water sports, including Red Cross water-safety classes, river tubing, trips to Pisgah Slide, a rope swing, and free swims each morning and afternoon.

With such a program, rigorous safety measures and solid staff experience are of utmost priority, and High Rocks has plenty of both. Many High Rocks counselors are former High Rocks campers; all are trained in CPR and have first aid certification. The camp has recently been accredited by The Association of Experiential Education, an organization that oversees adventure programs like Outward Bound and The National Outdoor Leadership School. Henry Birdsong, the camp director, is a former course director for Discovery, Inc., where he designed and directed outdoor adventure programs, and he has served on the staff of North Carolina Outward Bound School and Hurricane Island Outward Bound.

For campers who are interested in becoming counselors, High Rocks has an excellent counselor training program in which older campers work not only to improve their own skills but learn to teach them as well.

This camp doesn't change much. It is a known entity, a place where one can return year after year and find his expectations met. It's an informal, relaxed place where people are genuinely kind to one another. The founders and their children, who now run the camp, love young people and invest themselves completely and happily in their work. Their goal is for a boy to learn responsibility while he grows in self-confidence, and, from what I see, that is exactly what these boys are doing here.

Interlochen Arts Camp

Address:
P.O. Box 199
Interlochen, Michigan 49643-0199

Phone:
(616) 276-7472

Contact person:
Tom Bewley

Natural features:
Set between two glacial lakes in a pine forest

Nearest large city or town:
Traverse City

Enrollment:
Coed
Boys 37% Girls 63%

Age spread:
8–18

Per summer:
1,562

Campers come from the:
Northeast 12% Southeast 13% Central 43% Southwest 13% Northwest 7% International 12%

Average number of international campers:
158

Season:
June 26–August 22

Session (by percentage of campers) and cost:
4 weeks, 25%, $2,130
8 weeks, 75%, $3,550

Extra charges:
Some (supplies, lab fees, private lessons)

Scholarships:
25–30% of campers do not pay full tuition

Financial structure:
Independent, not for profit

Founded:
1927

Owner(s) and years associated with camp:
Interlochen Center for the Arts, 67

Managing Director(s) and years associated with camp:
Edward J. Downing, 16

Director's background:
Edward J. Downing: B.M., M.M., University of Michigan; Conductor, National High School Band; teacher, conductor at high school and college levels; administrator of all-state programs; toured Europe as conductor of youth groups

Counselors: 207
Men 42% Women 58% Min. age 18
Ratio to campers 1: 7

Health and safety:
3 infirmaries, 25 RNs, 2 doctors on staff

Concentration:
Intensive training in all kinds of music,
dance, visual art, theater arts; character and
leadership development

Mission:
"The mission of the Interlochen Center for the Arts is to offer gifted and talented young people
the opportunity to develop their creative abilities in a wholesome community under the guidance of an exemplary faculty of artists and educators."

Although this is technically a specialty camp, I could not in good conscience
leave Interlochen off any list of the country's best camps. After all, many
people consider this to be the very best fine-arts camp in the world, a place where
both the young artist and the potential artist can explore and develop their creative
abilities.

Like all good camps, Interlochen provides a nurturing environment, and that's
especially important here. Many of the gifted youngsters who come here are likely
to be unique people in their own schools. Here they can be with hundreds of
kindred souls. Of all the camps in this book, Interlochen probably represents the
most diverse geographical group of campers, drawing youngsters from all fifty states
and thirty-five other countries. And it also has the most active and generous scholarship program.

Affiliated with the University of Michigan, Interlochen is comprised of three
parts: Interlochen Arts Camp, Interlochen Arts Academy (an independent school
for the artistically gifted and talented), and Interlochen Public Radio, a National
Public Radio affiliate. During the summer, while camp is in session, the Interlochen Arts Festival hosts world-renowned performers in all areas of the performing
arts. Many of the artists serve as guest speakers and teachers for classes in the Arts
Camp, and many perform as part of the campers' ensembles.

The camp is located in the heart of Michigan's northern vacation country, set
between two clear-water glacial lakes in a pine forest. The facilities are in a class by
themselves, much more like a top-notch college campus than a summer camp.
Grounds are beautifully landscaped, and buildings and cabins blend easily into the
natural environment. But make no mistake. Campers don't come here to relax.
Interlochen offers concentrated, accelerated, and *highly competitive* programs in all

the arts, particularly music, taught by teachers and performers who are world-famous in their fields.

Over 250 courses are offered during the eight-week session, in four areas: music, art, dance, and theater. To illustrate the breadth of undertaking, this camp maintains 450 buildings on campus, housing 15,058 beds and more than 500 pianos! There are five orchestras, four bands, four choirs, and four jazz bands, which, along with dance, theater, and visual-art departments, present more than five hundred events every summer.

You might be afraid that a child would feel lost in such a place. But campers live in small groups with counselors who are hired more for their people skills than their artistic talent. These staff people provide the same kind of personal guidance and support as does the staff of any committed camp. Unlike the arts instructors who concentrate mainly in their specific fields, the counselors teach all the traditional camp activities and really get to know these youngsters.

Campers are divided by age into three divisions: elementary school campers in the Junior Division, junior high students in Intermediate, and the oldest campers in the High School Division. Juniors and Intermediate campers may choose to enroll for only a four-week session or may attend the full eight weeks. Campers spend most of their instructional time concentrating in their particular fields (arts activities are too numerous to list here but, believe me, nothing is overlooked).

Because the camp believes that all youngsters need a variety of experiences as well as character and leadership skills, the same priorities are valued here as at any of the other fine camps. And the same activities are offered: sailing, boating, canoeing, swimming, archery, campcraft, camping overnights, environmental trips, basketball, cross country, exercise class, Frisbee, Ping-Pong, soccer, softball, tennis, volleyball, and weight lifting.

State-of-the-art? Exemplary? Professional? Adjectives cannot describe this place. This is such an extraordinary summer camp, it would not be stretching the point to claim that Interlochen stands alone in its own league. Lots of big, important decisions are made by children here, often without their knowing it. The people who work with them are committed to their mission, they are perfectly focused, and they are superb.

Keewaydin Camps

(NOTE: This is one of ten Keewaydin Camps for boys, girls, and adults in Canada and the Northeast)

Address:
RR1, Box 88
Salisbury, Vermont 05769

Phone:
(802) 352-4247

Natural features:
Situated on Lake Dunmore; 500 acres of fields, woods, and a mountainside

Nearest large city or town:
Middlebury

Enrollment:
Boys

Age spread:
8–16

Per summer:
180

Campers come from the:
Northeast 89% Southeast 1% Central 1%
Northwest 1% Southwest 1% International 7%

Average number of international campers:
13—Venezuela 5, Germany 3, Spain 3

Season:
June 27–August 21

Session (by percentage of campers) and cost:
4 weeks, 45%, $2,700
8 weeks, 55%, $3,650

Extra charges:
None

Financial structure:
Private, not for profit

Founded:
1894

Owner(s) and years associated with camp:
The Keewaydin Foundation, 9

Managing Director(s) and years associated with camp:
Alfred G. Hare, Jr., 71
James Wacker, 3

Directors' backgrounds:
Alfred G. Hare, Jr.: graduate, University of Pennsylvania; started as a camper in 1923; moved to staff, owner, director

James Wacker: graduate, Otterbein College, Ohio; Executive Director, Keewaydin Foundation; will gradually replace Mr. Hare as director; Executive Director, Youth Homes in Mid-America, since 1977

Counselors: 55
Men 97% Women 3% Min. age 18
Ratio to campers 1: 3

Health and safety:
Infirmary, 2 RNs and doctor on staff

Concentration:
Canoeing is the hallmark; a wide variety of other activities includes sports, dramatics, arts and crafts

Mission:
"To provide children with the opportunity to grow in self-esteem and independence through outdoor experiences."

Keewaydin, located in the midst of the Green Mountains, Champlain Valley, and the Adirondacks, is the oldest private independent camp in the country. The fact that the vast campus encompasses an entire bay of Lake Dunmore as well as one side of adjacent Mt. Moosalamoo enhances the camp's ambitious tripping and waterfront programs.

Keewaydin boys are divided into four separate camps ("wigwams"), according to age, each camp maintaining its own location, director, and staff; its own waterfront, canoes and boats, play areas, lodge, library; and its own activities program. Campers live in tents and cabins, in small groups of three or four boys to one or two staffmen.

Despite the separation of age groups, all wigwams come together for meals in a wonderful old dining hall, a building rife with tradition. A birch-bark canoe is mounted on the wall, surrounded by college banners, flags of the campers' home countries, and plaques bearing the names of all the campers going back to 1900.

Keewaydin is best known for its tripping program, but instruction in other areas is first-rate, too. Each morning, with the help of his staffman, a boy will choose his day's activity from a list that includes swimming, diving, boating, canoeing, baseball, tennis, arts and crafts, sailing, soccer, and dramatics. Departing from the multiple-activity scheduling of most camps, Keewaydin schedules only one activity period each morning and afternoon, enabling a camper to really concentrate on his chosen skill.

Other activities regularly available include exploration/ecology, hiking, kayaking, photography, riflery and archery, wrestling and boxing, and white-water canoeing. Depending on the skills of the staffmen, wigwams may also learn fly-tying, orienteering, basketball, snorkeling, spelunking, fishing, lacrosse, mountaineering and rock climbing, or volleyball. A general swim is offered prior to each meal for those who want it, and during free periods boys may fish, play pickup sports, go canoeing, sailing, or boating, play tennis, read, play Ping-Pong or horseshoes, or work in the bug house. There are lots of evening games, too, and several special events, from Fourth of July fireworks to dances with nearby girls' camps.

Every Keewaydin camper goes on either a canoeing or hiking trip each month.

The youngest boys go out for two nights. Middle groups spend three to seven days on Lake George, Lake Champlain, the Connecticut River, or Vermont's Long Trail. And the oldest groups, in the Moosalamoo wigwam, spend three or four weeks either canoeing or hiking in New Hampshire's White Mountains, Maine's Rangeley Lakes, or New York's Adirondacks.

When a Keewaydin camper turns sixteen, if he's qualified and willing, he becomes eligible for the coveted five-week canoe trip into remote Canadian waters, where he lives with only his small group, a Cree Indian guide, and a two-way radio.

Smiles abound here. People seem to be genuinely excited about being with one another. This is the kind of place where everybody really gets to know everybody else, and it seems the more they get to know one another, the more they like each other. Keewaydin's counselors are among the most energetic I have seen, an open and friendly group committed to building their campers' self-esteem, and a group that returns to Keewaydin at a rate of 75 percent each year.

Over the raised boxing ring in the middle of camp is a banner that says, "The gold is not what is important. Training, participating, being a part of an event are the things that count. Winning is just the icing on the cake."

What counts to this camp is the growth of its campers. Keewaydin's mission is clear and understood by everyone, to the extent that everything they do is designed to fulfill that mission. Because the camp is operated by a nonprofit corporation with a self-perpetuating board of trustees, its educational services and the values it espouses will endure for a long time to come.

Camp Kieve

A Non-Profit Organization

Address:
P.O. Box 169
Nobleboro, Maine 04555

Phone:
(207) 563-5172
Fax (207) 563-5215

Natural features:
Situated on a hilltop peninsula of Damariscotta Lake, with three miles of frontage and
300 acres of mostly woods; near the seacoast

Nearest large city or town:
Damariscotta

Enrollment:
Boys

Age spread:
8–16

Per summer:
350 (160 per session)

Campers come from the:
Northeast 62% Southeast 15% Central 10%
Northwest 1% Southwest 4% International
8%

**Average number of international
campers:**
33—Germany 12, France 5, Italy 4, England
3, Venezuela 3, Colombia 2, Philippines 2

Season:
June 21–August 13

**Session (by percentage of campers)
and cost:**
3¹/₂ weeks, 98%, $2,350
7 weeks, 2%, $4,700

Extra charges:
Some (uniform, optional tutoring, long
trips)

Scholarships:
10% of campers do not pay full tuition

Financial structure:
Private, not for profit

Founded
1926

**Owner(s) and years associated with
camp:**
Kieve Affective Education, Inc., 69

**Managing Director(s) and years asso-
ciated with camp:**
Henry R. Kennedy, 20

**Other Director(s) and years associated
with camp:**
Charles Richardson, 12
Jared Schott, 8

Directors' backgrounds:
Henry R. Kennedy: B.A., Colby College;
camper and counselor at Kieve from 1967–
80; trustee 1984–89

Charles Richardson: B.A., Bates College;
teacher and coach for 8 years

Jared Schott: B.A., Bates College; teacher
and coach for 3 years

Counselors: 52
Men 76% Women 24% Min. age 18
Ratio to campers 1: 3

Concentration:
Noncompetitive; wilderness trips and a wide
variety of in-camp activities and sports

Health and safety:
Infirmary, RN on staff; doctor on call; hospital 7 miles away

Mission:
"To affect the lives of young people by creating a variety of experiences that will increase their
self-confidence and trust, and, consequently, their capacity to give to others."

Kieve is a beautiful camp occupying an entire hilltop peninsula of Damariscotta Lake, on the Maine seacoast. Surrounded by nearly three miles of
sandy lakefront and located at the end of a long country road in a quaint coastal
town, the camp provides 130 boys with an enviable mix of ocean, fresh water, and
wilderness experiences. It's a place filled with the age-old sounds of a lakeside
summer, from the cheerful shouts of boys' voices to the distant pealing of chimes
summoning the community to a new event.

A multitude of fine buildings are sensibly spread over the property to give the
campus a woodsy, spacious feel. There is a wonderful main lodge which houses a
grand stone fireplace and performance stage, a library, a large multi-purpose building for basketball and other games, and an arts building that contains a modern
darkroom, several pottery wheels, a printing press, a ceramics studio, and a fine
woodworking shop.

The dining hall at Kieve is one of those places that brings an old camper back
to his boyhood. With high ceilings and tall, screened windows, the place is charged
with the energy of hungry boys who have been hard at play. They sit six to a table
with two counselors and share most mealtimes with the former director and his
wife, who live on the edge of the premises.

Among the camp's outdoors facilities are two grassy playing fields, four all-
weather tennis courts, archery and rifle ranges, and a state-of-the-art ropes course
located in the fringes of a pine forest. The beach is sandy, the lake water comfortable and clean, and Kieve's fleet of over forty canoes, Windsurfers, and sailboats is
large enough to accommodate every boy there.

Campers sleep in eight cabins located on the hillside overlooking the lake. Each cabin group of twelve to fourteen boys is assigned to two activities in the morning, assuring that by the end of the week all boys will have been exposed to each activity offered at Kieve. In the afternoon every camper chooses the activity he wants to concentrate on.

Kieve's underlying philosophy is that a minimum of rules, balanced by a large number of understanding counselors and a program emphasizing free choice and deemphasizing competition, gives the group and the individual their best chance of success. Here each boy works his way up a ladder of well-defined skills in a number of experiences, including printing, photography, ceramics, deep-water sailing, riflery, archery, tennis, swimming, sailing, canoeing, woodworking, shop, fishing, outdoor skills, mountain climbing, nature, land sports, windsurfing, pottery, art, drama, music, and white-water rafting.

Above all, this is a camp that places a premium on getting its campers out of camp, whether on day trips or a variety of overnight camping trips. Every fair day, one cabin group or another goes out on Kieve's thirty-six-foot lobster boat, exploring the sea life around some of Maine's many islands, visiting an Audubon Society Museum on Hog Island, or maybe fishing for mackerel. Other groups may climb beautiful Mount Battie to look down on Penobscot Bay or just spend the afternoon playing at an ocean beach; while still others board a twenty-five-foot Friendship Sloop to learn deep-sea nautical skills from Kieve's master sailing instructor.

Every camper, regardless of age, spends at least three nights on trips. As boys get older, the trips get longer and more demanding. While a young boy's trip may take him to a nearby island for a couple of nights, the oldest boy may spend up to three weeks canoeing and hiking up in Allagash country or scaling Katahdin, Maine's highest mountain.

Parents, alumni, and friends of Kieve are always welcome at camp and have at their disposal a lovely four-bedroom cottage with private beach, dock, sailboat, and canoes. Guests are encouraged to participate in camp activities and are invited to Sunday's noontime outdoor chapel service and the luncheon that follows.

This is as good a camp as you'll find anywhere and a perfect example of the kind of institution with a rock-solid structure that will endure for generations to come. It is a nonprofit educational foundation, governed by a self-perpetuating board of trustees, fueled by a dedicated group of friends and alumni, and currently beginning its third generation of directors from the founding Kennedy family. Coupled with three assistant directors and their wives—all educators—this is the strongest administrative team I've seen. And Kieve's commitment to education is further bolstered by week-long Leadership Decisions Institutes, which run throughout the year, helping youngsters build self-esteem, values clarification, and decision-making skills.

To see a busload of campers return to camp after a demanding week in the woods and to hear the loud cheers welcoming them home is to understand this camp. Kieve exudes happiness. The traditions that have been carefully preserved over the years continue to work because they promote self-confidence and a feeling of belonging to a close-knit group.

A popular grace offered at dinner is: "Let us be ever mindful of the needs and feelings of others." During the meal, when campers' daily accomplishments are recognized with cheers, all of the boys become winners. Under the loud, informal tone of Kieve is a belief in the importance of each individual and the ever-present mission that each boy learn to take care of himself so that he can eventually be the kind of person that others will turn to for support.

Killooleet

Killooleet

Summer address:
Hancock, Vermont 05740-0070

Phone:
(802) 767-3152

Winter address:
15 Sarah Sanford Road, West
Bridgewater, CT 06752-1413

Phone:
(203) 354-5728

Natural features:
300 acres of woods and meadow on a private lake, set on the edge of the Green Mountain National Forest

Nearest large city or town:
35 miles northeast of Rutland, in the center of Vermont

Enrollment:
Coed

Age spread:
9–14

Per summer:
100

Season:
June 29–August 20

Session (by percentage of campers) and cost:
7¹/₂ weeks, 100%, $3,700

Extra charges:
None

Scholarships:
6% of campers do not pay full tuition

Financial structure:
For profit

Founded:
1927

Owners/Managers and years associated with camp:
Seeger family, 48

Director(s) and years associated with camp:
Katherine (Kate) Seeger, 39

Other Director(s) and years associated with camp:
John Seeger, 48
Eleanor Seeger, 48

Directors' backgrounds:
Katherine (Kate) Seeger: B.A. degree; 5th grade teacher; musician; ACA standards visitor with NE Section; camp director for 5 years

John Seeger: B.S., Harvard; M.A. and Ed.D., New York University; former school teacher and principal; former camp head counselor and codirector

Eleanor Seeger: B.A., Queens College; M.A., New York University; former teacher, college professor, camp head counselor and codirector

Counselors: 26
Men 54% Women 46% Min. age 18
Ratio to campers 1: 4

Health and safety:
Nurse and assistant nurse in residence; hospital 20 miles away

Concentration:
Noncompetitive camp program stressing individual growth and relationships

Mission:
 "We want each camper to find out what he or she likes to do, and to specialize in it. A child works hardest in areas she delights in. Camp is non-competitive, highly individual. Ninety-five percent of campers return until they're too old. This is their family, where they 'find themselves.' "

The entrance to Killooleet is a long, well-tended driveway that winds through tall trees beside a mountain stream. The campus is green, level, and freshly mowed, surrounded by farms and meadows and towering, rolling hills. If you've ever seen a Vermont country village in July, you get the picture.

Killooleet's facilities, both practical and well-maintained, exude a studied casualness, emphasizing the things that are most important here: the children and the natural beauty surrounding them. With a half-mile-long campus and facilities spread out from one end to the other, campers are encouraged to bring their bikes to camp and ride from place to place. Bicycles abound. So do dogs.

"We have a mature staff," states the camp catalog. "Each counselor runs his cabin and activity in a manner consistent with his personality and beliefs. Likewise, each child senses our faith in his individuality."

This is a successful experiment in promoting inner happiness by giving choices to children and trusting their decisions, always within carefully set bounds. For campers, a fine balance is struck between having to try all the activities and being able to choose a concentration. Killooleet offers a wide choice from a menu that balances sports and creative activities (all programs are gender-blind.) Craft and wood shops are homes to activities like leather, textiles, jewelry, stained glass, ceramics, and woodworking. There is another studio for drawing, painting, constructions, linoleum carving, statues, and mobiles. Simple indoor and outdoor stages provide space for dramatics, and each summer a musical and several shorter cabin productions are performed.

Music is big at Killooleet (American folk song vanguard Pete Seeger is related to these Seegers), with a camp chorus and various music ensembles. Guitar, banjo, dulcimer, and harmonica are taught, and there's always lots of singing in camp.

There are also nature studies and opportunities to experiment with electronics, rocketry, model airplanes, and kites. Campers learn to write and produce their own videos in and out of a simple production studio. There is even a course in mechanics, with go-carts available.

Sports activities include swimming, canoeing, kayaking, windsurfing, sailing, tennis, archery, riflery, gymnastics, softball, track, soccer, and sometimes fencing, lacrosse, basketball, mountaineering, and volleyball. Ten horses are available for the riding program, where children learn to care for the horses and ride English style as they progress to trail rides, dressage, and jumping.

At the end of the second week, every cabin group goes on a three-day camping trip. During the sixth week, campers may elect to go on much more demanding trips.

Well-founded and well-run, Killooleet is confident, principled, and a very successful institution that will last far into the future because of the solid dedication of the leadership and staff to the camp's mission. The camp is always full, with only a 30 percent turnover in campers and staff each year.

The directors are first and foremost imaginative, committed educators. As one director explains, "The community supports creative risk-takers; this gives them courage." That attitude infuses both staff and campers alike with a wonderful creative energy and initiative. Particularly satisfying is watching the older campers pass on to the younger ones things they have learned at camp.

Killooleet was founded on the belief that what a child thinks and how he or she feels is *always* important. Since all campers feel valued, they find it easy to live happily and cooperatively with one another. The chain reaction of goodwill and supportiveness began with the Seegers' vision, and it has been maintained and enriched by members of this community ever since. Nontraditional in the sense that they have no camp song, camp colors, or cheers, Killooleet has nurtured its own tradition in the last 68 years—and that's the most enduring lesson to all who come here.

Kingsley Pines Camp

Address:
RFD 1, Plains Road
Raymond, Maine 04071

Phone:
(207) 655-7181

Natural features:
Lakeside location; sandy beach, sandy bottom

Nearest large city or town:
Lewiston, Auburn

Enrollment:
Coed
Boys 50% Girls 50%

Age spread:
7–16

Per summer:
210

Campers come from the:
Northeast 35% Southeast 20% Central 15%
Northwest 5% Southwest 5% International
20%

Average number of international campers:
14—France 5, England 4

Season:
June 28–August 9

Session (by percentage of campers) and cost:
3 weeks, 50%, $1,995
6 weeks, 50%, $3,595

Extra charges:
Very little (transportation from airport, if requested)

Scholarships:
30% of campers do not pay full tuition

Financial structure:
For profit

Founded:
1929

Owner(s) and years associated with camp:
Pat Coughlin, 11

Managing Director(s) and years associated with camp:
Jake Congleton, 11

Other Director(s) and years associated with camp:
Sally Congleton, 11

Directors' backgrounds:
Jake Congleton: B.A., Wesleyan; M.B.A., Harvard; M.A., University of London; former dean, teacher, coach; 36 years at Camp Timanous as associate director, waterfront director and program director

Sally Congleton: B.S.—RN, Virginia Commonwealth; FPN, Northeastern; head of health center; camp nurse

Counselors: 50
Men 50% Women 50% Min. age 17
Ratio to campers 1: 3

Health and safety:
Infirmary, RN and LPN on staff; hospital nearby

Concentration:
Broad range of activities centering on children's growth and development

Mission:
"Commitment to coeducation, healthy food and activities, and traditional camp values."

Kingsley Pines is a coed camp that is so informal and relaxed its careful organization is almost invisible. Located on Panther Lake in the lakes region of southern Maine, the campus rests on seventy acres of beautiful lakefront property that is surrounded by pine forests and mountains. Lawns and playing fields are carefully maintained, and facilities are thoughtfully laid out so the campus is neat and accessible while still retaining a natural, woodsy atmosphere.

But what sets Kingsley Pines apart from other coed camps is its commitment to reaching as diverse a group of youngsters—both geographically and economically—as possible. The camp accomplishes this with both a generous scholarship program and ambitious recruiting of campers from other countries.

Kingsley Pines' facilities include a sandy-bottomed waterfront area complete with ten swimming lanes and a diving float. The fleet consists of classic wood and canvas canoes, along with modern fiberglass canoes, sailboats, rowboats, pedal boats, Windsurfers, rowing shells, and a water-ski boat. The camp has a fine central recreation lodge and a superb performing arts building. Other facilities include a fully equipped wood shop, arts building, music studio, dance studio, photography lab, computer center, nature center, and lakeside tennis courts. A pleasant dining hall overlooks the lake, and whenever the weather permits, campers eat outside.

Boys and girls live in separate sections of the camp, in cabins that house from three to eight campers, supervised by one to three counselors, with separate bathroom and shower facilities. Living arrangements aside, this is one camp that is truly gender-neutral in its offerings to boys and girls, who participate together in all activities and on all trips.

Kingsley Pines strives to balance formal instruction with recreational activities each day. "We want to make the kids feel good about themselves by offering new challenges and positively reinforcing their successes," says owner Pat Coughlin, who is also an active participant in the camp's functioning.

While campers are able to choose their own activities, they are encouraged to experience all the activities the camp has to offer. Each camper takes a complete Red Cross swimming program at his or her own skill level, and every boy and girl is taught sailing, windsurfing, canoeing, and rowing. Other activities from which campers may choose include tennis, campcraft, nature, shop, photography, computers, ecology, baseball, soccer, non-contact lacrosse, waterskiing, music, and drama, as well as both day-trips and overnight campouts. In addition (and for additional fees), Kingsley Pines offers English, French, and Spanish as second languages or tutoring in any subject for those campers requiring additional preparation for school (none of these academics interferes with the normal camp schedule, however).

Another feature that sets Kingsley Pines apart are the parents' cabins, which enable a camper's parents to stay on campus ($50–$80 per night, meals included) for up to three days—and not only observe but participate in many of the activities with their child. Following the regular camp season, Kingsley Pines offers a week of family camp as well.

This is a happy place, quietly purposeful and very well organized, built on sound, traditional values. Although boys and girls this age sometimes have relationships that are tense or frivolous, at this camp the boys and girls seem to be comfortable with one another. I suspect that has something to do with the simple, unfettered setting in which they find themselves. Without a doubt, it has a lot to do with the camp's experienced and devoted director, Jake Congleton, and his positive staff, who are always mindful of the benefits of giving lots of praise. In such a supportive atmosphere, it becomes difficult for any of these youngsters to feel bad about themselves or, as a consequence, each other.

Camp Longhorn

Address:
Box 60
Burnet, Texas 78611

Phone:
(512) 793-2811

Natural features:
Located in Texas Hill Country, on Inks
Lake

Nearest large city or town:
50 miles northwest of Austin

Enrollment:
Coed
Boys 45% Girls 55%

Age spread:
7–15

Per summer:
1,812

Campers come from the:
Northeast 1% Southeast 1% Central 2%
Northwest 1% Southwest 95%

Season:
June 2–August 12

**Session (by percentage of campers)
and cost:**
2 weeks, 25%, $1,156.70
3 weeks, 75%, $1,554.30

Extra charges:
Some

Scholarships:
5% of campers do not pay full tuition

Financial structure:
For profit

Founded:
1939

**Owner(s) and years associated with
camp:**
Robertson family, 55

**Managing Director(s) and years asso-
ciated with camp:**
Tex Robertson, 55

**Other Director(s) and years associated
with camp:**
Pat Robertson, 55
John Robertson, 43

Directors' backgrounds:
Tex Robertson: B.S., University of Texas

Pat Robertson: B.A., Southern Methodist
University

John Robertson: B.A., Southwestern Texas
University

Counselors: 136
Men 48% Women 52% Min. age 17
Ratio to campers 1: 4

Health and safety:
Infirmary, 4 RNs on staff, MD on staff;
hospital 13 miles away

Concentration:
Health and safety, cabin unit friendship, love
of camp life, happiness, compatibility,
sportsmanship, activities, positive attitude

Mission:
"To provide the most valuable experience for a lifetime. To make people sure of themselves and anxious to help others. Camp slogan: Everybody is Somebody at Camp Longhorn."

The minute you enter the one mile entrance to this camp you are bombarded by silly signs: "George Bush on right" next to a bush with a "George" sign, or "Don't cross creek if sign is underwater." The signs prepare you for an institution that is at once proud but also able to laugh at itself. In short, Longhorn is infested with good, wholesome Texas fun. Shoes may or may not be on feet, shorts may not be pressed or perfectly clean, but it's next to impossible to find one person who doesn't love this place.

Camp Longhorn is a big Texas camp on a big Texas lake. And all the best things you've ever heard about Texas come true here. Everywhere you go you find warm, generous people who are completely honest with one another. There is absolutely no pretense in this place. Self-deprecating humor is the rule. As we walk through the camp with the eighty-five-year-old founder, everybody calls out, "Hi, Tex!" and we invariably stop for a moment so they can joke together.

In such an atmosphere, it's easy to see that Longhorn's emphasis is on close personal relationships. "Cabin cohesion" and "cabin spirit" are key phrases. With a thousand people present at any given time, such a small-group system, and small-group spirit, works remarkably well. Campers live twelve to each two-story cabin, along with three counselors. Some teen-age campers live on floating cabins.

Activities offered here include swimming, rappelling, gymnastics, diving, sailing, archery, trampoline, riflery, horseback riding, waterskiing, canoeing, wildlife, pickleball, water polo, craftwork, tennis, soccer, blobbing, fishing, scuba diving, lifesaving, Olympic swim, baseball, and windsurfing. Additional activities for girls include water ballet, singing, cheerleading, volleyball, and kickball. For boys: pistolry, basketball, football, and tumbling. Older campers have a more advanced swimming program, with more concentration on other water activities. Teenage campers use Inks Lake for advanced sailing, windsurfing, and waterskiing.

The evening schedule provides for a dance night, a feature movie, and a Sunday church service each week. Other special events, team competitions, and "free and easy times" are added into the schedule throughout the week.

Campers are given three fine meals in the Chow Hall each day, along with mid-morning and mid-afternoon snacks. They eat cafeteria-style, choose their own seats, and clean their own trays in an atmosphere that is informal, noisy, and just as happy as the rest of camp life.

Perhaps the thing that best illustrates Longhorn's educational philosophy of motivational rewards is the camp store, called the Merit Store. Campers are not allowed to bring money to camp, but whenever a camper does something meritorious, any of the staff will reward him or her with wampum, which is Longhorn's currency and with which store items may be purchased.

Camp Longhorn's population is made up mostly of Texans, but that doesn't seem to present a problem: Texas is so big that many of these boys and girls live hundreds of miles apart. Besides, there really isn't much room for anyone else or much need for Longhorn to go out recruiting. There's a long backlist of youngsters waiting to get in. Even so, every boy and girl who comes here is personally interviewed before being placed in one of the three 3-week or one 2-week sessions.

This is a grand old camp built on years of tradition, and a very large camp that maintains as friendly an atmosphere as even the smallest camps I've visited. The standards in practice for many years will no doubt endure for a long time to come, as Longhorn is already owned by the next generation of Robertsons. The counselors here are absolutely devoted, both to the campers and to the spirit of the camp. They eat, sleep, and play with the youngsters in their care. Most were former Longhorn campers themselves, selected as older campers and trained under supervision of senior counselors and directors. Remarkably, 88 percent return year after year, a real measure of this camp's value.

Camp Maxwelton (For Boys)

Camp Lachlan (For Girls)

Summer address:
Box 107
Rockbridge Baths, Virginia 24473

Phone:
(703) 348-5757

Winter address:
Box 98
Rockbridge Baths, VA 24473

Phone:
(703) 348-1090

Natural features:
Located on Walkers Creek; part of a 300-acre farm at the foot of Jump Mountain. A lake is on the campus.

Nearest large city or town:
Lexington

Enrollment:
Boys' camp and girls' camp run at separate times

Age spread:
Boys 9–15; Girls 8–15

Per summer:
160

Campers come from the:
Northeast 2% Southeast 94% Central 2% Other 2%

Season:
Boys: mid June to late July

First-year boys (9 and 10 years old):
June 18–July 9
Girls: July 30–August 19

Session (by percentage of campers) and cost:
Boys' 3 weeks, 15%, $1,075
Boys' 5 weeks, 85%, $1,395
Girls' 3 weeks, 100%, $1,055

Extra charges:
None

Financial structure:
For profit

Founded:
Maxwelton 1949; Lachlan 1954

Owner(s) and years associated with camp:
McLaughlin family, 46

Managing Director(s) and years associated with camp:
Lee M. McLaughlin, Jr., 41
Nancy F. McLaughlin, 28

Directors' backgrounds:
Lee M. McLaughlin, Jr.: M. Ed., educational administration and supervision, University of Virginia; teacher, coach, administrator

Nancy F. McLaughlin: educator; mother of three

Counselors:
Maxwelton
Men 100% Min. age 16
Ratio to campers 1: 4½
Lachlan
Men 10% Women 90% Min. age 16
Ratio to campers 1: 4½

Health and safety:
Infirmary; MDs make routine visits; clinic
12 minutes away

Concentration:
Activities include horseback riding, swimming, riflery, tennis, team sports, crafts, drama, dance, and fishing

Mission:
"It is our belief that young people can best grow and develop in a wholesome Christian atmosphere. Our aim is to aid in building the character of our campers, and day-to-day Christian living is emphasized."

Maxwelton and Lachlan are camps that believe that a group of young people are at their best when they act like a well-regulated family. And this, more than any camp I've seen, is a family camp.

The campus is situated on a three-hundred-acre farm at the base of a mountain. This is lovely, prosperous farmland with a river flowing quietly through the camp and a lake that is fed by mountain springs. Walking around the campus, you sometimes hear nothing more than the singing of songbirds or, occasionally, a distant bugle blowing a call to breakfast or dinner.

The dining room is part of the main house, a gracious old nineteenth-century Southern home graced by flowering shrubs and attractive pathways. Inside walls are adorned with pictures of each group of campers since Maxwelton was founded in 1949. During meals the old family dog snoozes at his master's feet, and conversations are personal and caring. The atmosphere is one of simple dignity, buoyed by happiness. When there is a decision to be made, everybody present is encouraged to provide input, but the final decision is left to the director. And that same large-family spirit extends all through camp life.

Campers and staff sing together, and they celebrate their visitors with a cheer. Every morning there are daily devotions that are light but always sincere and meaningful. It's almost as if this place were a small retreat, deliberately sealed off from the rest of the world. I have a feeling that the directors and campers alike are well aware of this and intend for it to stay that way.

Maxwelton boys occupy the campus for the first part of the summer, and

Lachlan girls take over for three weeks at the end of July. Although the girls do many of the same things that the boys do, activity programs differ in traditional ways. For example, where girls are offered field hockey, dance, tumbling, and drama, boys' activities tend to be more sports-oriented, such as wrestling, golf, football, and skeet shooting. Activities offered to both boys and girls include horseback riding, tennis, swimming, volleyball, riflery, arts and crafts, archery, lacrosse, soccer, and other team games.

Campers live in solid, screened-in cabins set on a hillside that commands a sweeping view of the surrounding countryside and the camp's spring-fed lake. Counselors, most of whom are former Maxwelton/Lachlan campers, return to their camp each summer at the rate of approximately 75 percent, which is a strong indication that the McLaughlins are doing a lot of things right.

There is a quiet spirituality about this camp, tempered with a warm sense of humor, the kind of feeling that loving families aspire to. By mixing age groups, such a family concept is enhanced. It's the kind of place where a fourteen-year-old boy offers to take a nine-year-old boy fishing—because they're brothers. In such an environment, which combines modest facilities with a deep and humane philosophy, there is no doubt in my mind that these camps will continue in their unassuming way to enhance the lives of young men and women for many years to come.

Camp Merrie-Woode

Address:
100 Merrie-Woode Road
Sapphire, North Carolina 28774

Phone:
(704) 743-3300

Natural features:
Located on mile-long, privately owned Lake Fairfield at the base of a 1,000-foot rock face in the mountains of southwestern North Carolina

Nearest large city or town:
An hour and 15 minutes southwest of Asheville, near the northern borders of Georgia and South Carolina

Enrollment:
Girls

Age spread:
7–16

Per summer:
540 (180 per session)

Campers come from the:
Southeast 90% Northeast 5% Other Areas 5%

Season:
June 4–August 18

Session and cost:
2 weeks (June), $940
5 weeks (Main), $2,085
3 weeks (August), $1,365

Extra charges:
Very little (uniforms only)

Scholarships:
3% of campers do not pay full tuition

Financial structure:
Private, not for profit

Founded:
1919

Owner(s) and years associated with camp:
Merrie-Woode Foundation, 43

Managing Director(s) and years associated with camp:
Gordon Strayhorn, 5
Laurie Strayhorn, 5

Other Director(s) and years associated with camp:
Sid Long, 9

Directors' backgrounds:
Gordon Strayhorn: B.A., Indiana University; former camp counselor and assistant director; high school English teacher at boarding school for girls

Laurie Strayhorn: former Merrie-Woode camper; waterfront counselor; high school English teacher and dorm parent at boarding school for girls

Sid Long: managed camp office and books; oversaw counselors and camp program

Counselors: 65
Men 10% Women 90% Min. age 19
Ratio to campers 1: 3

Health and safety:
Infirmary, 1 or 2 RNs on campus at all hours; most often a visiting doctor lives on campus; medical center 4 miles away

Concentration:
Canoeing, kayaking, hiking, backpacking, rock climbing, weaving, studio arts and crafts, drama, other general camp activities

Mission:
"Merrie-Woode is a camp based on Christian tradition. We hope that campers will learn a variety of skills and as a result grow in their self-confidence. We also want them to learn to form a variety of friendships and to live in a community that emphasizes service, caring and consideration of others."

This is a girls' camp grounded in traditional camping activities and traditional values. Situated on a private lake and surrounded by several fine white-water rivers, it is a perfect place for canoeing and kayaking, programs in which this camp excels. In fact, many of the country's top women paddlers got their starts at Merrie-Woode.

The camp's location at the base of a thousand-foot rock face, and surrounded by the Blue Ridge Mountains, provides an ideal setting for its extensive mountaineering program. Backpacking is a constant feature of Merrie-Woode camp life, with three- to five-day trips going out of camp continuously.

The campus, enjoying its seventy-seventh continuous year as a girls' camp, is spaciously built along a half mile of shoreline. Spread out among the hemlock trees, rhododendron, and flowering laurel are several chestnut-sided lodges with stone chimneys, while thirty-eight cabins wind along the lake shore, each housing four girls and one counselor.

Counselors at Merrie-Woode are noticably mature; some are married and live on campus with their spouses (who are also Merrie-Woode counselors), enhancing the family spirit of the camp. Although all staff are kept refreshed by taking one day a week off away from camp (as well as many other free times during the week), all campers are monitored closely and have very little unstructured or unsupervised time.

The variety of noncompetitive camp activities includes archery, soccer, photography, ceramics, drama, horseback riding, and tennis. Among the studio arts offerings is weaving, an activity not often found in camps. Girls in the five-week session rehearse and perform a full-length musical production.

Merrie-Woode's canoeing and kayaking program deserves additional mention. Started 57 years ago, the program has evolved into a five-level skill-building progression that takes many of the girls four or five summers to work through the ranks. The entire waterfront program is enhanced by three beautifully maintained docks on the lake.

All facilities are excellent in form and function. A lodge called Castle is large enough to house the entire Merrie-Woode population for camp meetings and evening programs. Equipped with a stage and curtain, it is also the site of theater productions. On a hill behind Castle is a new gym equipped with a climbing wall. Across from the gym are three tennis courts.

The camp strives for diversity in its population, both geographic and racial. Campers and staff alike seem to prize their camp. Seventy-five percent return each year, and many counselors are former campers. The three sessions (often filled by November) each have their own rationale. The two-week program serves as an introduction to Merrie-Woode camping for younger girls, while the main session, from late June through early August, has the most depth and attracts the largest number of older campers.

Dining at Merrie-Woode is family style, with six campers and two counselors at each table in the large, log-built dining hall. Meals, prepared in a brand-new, state-of-the-art kitchen, are wholesome and largely homemade, consisting of many fresh fruits and vegetables. An ample salad bar is provided at every lunch and dinner.

This is a stable institution tucked away in some of the most beautiful land in the country, an ideal site for Merrie-Woode's special mission. There is no pretense here, but rather an open, friendly atmosphere, a place that doesn't mind its campers getting a little dirty in order to test themselves in a new adventure. Structurally, the institution is sound and well managed, owned and operated by a board of trustees, who are all former Merrie-Woode campers, and their families. Together with the administrative staff, counselors, and campers, these people share both a common purpose and an uncommon pride in their community.

Camp Mondamin (For Boys)

Green Cove (For Girls)

MONDAMIN
TUXEDO, NORTH CAROLINA
28784

Address:
Mondamin
P.O. Box 8
Tuxedo, North Carolina 28784

Green Cove
P.O. Box 38
Tuxedo, North Carolina 28784

Phone:
(704) 692-6355

Natural features:
Located on Lake Summit, bordering Pisgah National Forest, with fields and many miles of trails

Nearest large city or town:
Asheville

Enrollment:
Mondamin: Boys
Green Cove: Girls

Age spread:
7–17

Per summer:
Mondamin: 400
Green Cove: 360
(180–200 per session)

Campers come from the:
Mondamin:
Northeast 6% Southeast 78% Central 5% Northwest 1% Southwest 7% International 3%

Green Cove:
Northeast 7% Southeast 75% Central 5% Northwest 1% Southwest 6% International 6%

Average number of international campers:
Mondamin: 14—Venezuela 9, France 3

Green Cove: 16—Venezuela 15

Season:
June 8–August 25

Session (by percentage of campers) and cost:
1 week, 5%, $375
3 weeks, 50%, $1,450
6½ weeks, 45%, $3,100

Extra charges:
Very few

Scholarships:
4% of campers do not pay full tuition

Financial structure:
For profit

Founded:
Mondamin: 1922
Green Cove: 1945

Owner(s) and years associated with camp:
Bell family, 73

Managing Director(s) and years associated with camp:
Mondamin:
Frank D. Bell, Jr., 33

Green Cove:
Nancy M. Bell, 31

Directors' backgrounds:
Frank D. Bell, Jr.: B.A., Wesleyan University; 21 years camp director

Nancy M. Bell: B.A., Randolph-Macon Woman's College; M.A.T., Emory University; teacher; 13 years camp director

Counselors: 105
Men 48% Women 52% Min. age 18
Ratio to Campers 1: 3$^{1}/_{2}$

Health and safety:
Infirmary, 2 RNs and a doctor on staff;
hospital nearby

Concentration:
Swimming, kayaking, canoeing, tennis, riding, sailing, backpacking, rock climbing, ropes course, mountain biking, many trips

Mission:
"Our goal is to educate children through adventure, which is activity on one's personal frontier. We encourage independence and self-discipline; we work to enhance self-esteem and initiative. The atmosphere is non-competitive, the better to reduce pressure and to encourage experimentation with new ideas and skills; and it is structured but non-regimented, the better to promote thought, initiative and self-direction."

More than a few southeasterners look back at Mondamin and Green Cove as second homes, having spent many of their childhood summers here. In fact, these two camps, situated on opposite shores of Lake Summit, are the proud grandparents of all camps in North Carolina (twenty of which are currently operated by former Mondamin/Green Cove campers and counselors).

Although many summer residences have grown up around Mondamin over the years, Green Cove remains off by itself on the upper end of the lake and still feels remote and spacious. Both camps are bedrocks of tradition, professionally run and deeply committed. Their program, philosophy, and leadership are well founded and well tested over the years.

"We believe that young people need roots and they need wings," states the camp brochure, "and that neither is much good without the other. We try to allow as much freedom as a child can wisely use. He will have the opportunity for choice, along with guidance in making those choices."

Both camps offer three sessions: June Camp (three weeks, for ages 7–15), Main Camp (6$^{1}/_{2}$ weeks, for ages 8–17), and August Camp (one week, for ages 6–10).

The activities at both camps center around water, woods, and horses. Adventure is emphasized. Campers choose their own activities and learn to be responsible for themselves in a nurturing, noncompetitive atmosphere. Age is not a requirement for any activity or trip; each camper progresses at his or her own rate. Although the boys' and girls' camps do some things together—sailing, for instance, and a few days trips and a weekly "social"—for the most part, boys stay with boys, and girls stay with girls.

Boys and girls from both camps are encouraged to set goals for themselves in roughly three activities and then to pursue them to excellence. The boys of Mondamin lean toward mountaineering, rock climbing, and white-water canoeing. While the girls of Green Cove also participate in those activities, more emphasis is placed on riding. The camp has thirty horses, four rings, several fields, a cross-country course, and miles of trails, in addition to crafts (weaving, pottery, macrame, painting, tie-dying, batiking, etc.) and tennis (four courts).

Both Mondamin and Green Cove enjoy active and varied tripping programs. A page from a recent summer's daily log reads: "Tuesday—The Mondamin Barons went to Pisgah Slides—at 5 o'clock in the morning! A rock-climbing trip went to Capp's Rock, and a tubing trip went down the Green. A one-day Nantahala canoeing trip left right after breakfast. A Mondamin sailing group exchanged with a Green Cove group at Lake Jocassee to stay out for four days. 'Recon' left later in the morning for a three-day canoe trip on the upper French Broad. The bus took two Green Cove hiking trips to the Smokies and a Mondamin climbing trip to Devil's Courthouse. The Nature Lab took a field trip."

Evening activities are nearly as varied. Many nights the campers gather around their campfires for stories and songs while one or more cabin groups set out on a cabin overnight. Other evenings might include games or special events like skit night or a special interest night, where campers share their hobbies and interests with each other. There are movies one night a week, and on Saturday there's a coed square dance or some other event that combines both camps.

"Our aim is to have stimulating counselors with time to explore and swap ideas with growing, curious campers," one of the camp brochures explains. "A real university can indeed be a log with a child on one end and an adult on the other."

The counselors at both camps are both friends and teachers to the campers. In total, this is a wonderfully devoted staff, most of whom were campers here in their younger years. Counselors live in a cabin with four to six campers and teach activities during the day.

Well-balanced meals in ample quantities are served family-style, with salad bars offered twice daily and fresh fruits always available. Fried foods and sweets are served, but not to excess. Candy and soft drinks are not available through machines or at the camp store.

"Learning to make decisions takes practice and will surely mean some mistakes," says Green Cove director Nancy Bell. "The camp atmosphere is a safe place to take some risks, fail, and try again." And that nurturing, noncompetitive atmosphere is exactly what these camps have provided for seventy years. When it comes to real-life education, it's easy to see that these people really know what they are doing.

Camp Onaway

Summer address:
Star Route 1
Box 1140
Bristol, New Hampshire 03222

Phone:
(603) 744-2180

Winter address:
1 Fogg Farm Road
Freeport, ME 04032

Phone:
(207) 865-4602

Natural features:
40-acre point of land on Newfound Lake

Nearest large city or town:
Laconia, Plymouth, Bristol

Enrollment:
Girls

Age spread:
9–16

Per summer:
82

Campers come from the:
Northeast 75% Southeast 15% Central 5%
Northwest 5%

Season:
June 24–August 13

Session (by percentage of campers) and cost:
7 weeks, 100%, $3,350

Extra charges:
Some (uniforms; hut trip)

Scholarships:
25% of campers do not pay full tuition

Financial structure:
Private, not for profit

Founded:
1911

Owner(s) and years associated with camp:
Onaway Camp Trust, 29

Managing Director(s) and years associated with camp:
Caroline Southall, 43

Director's background:
Caroline Southall: A.A., Colby Junior College; B.S.-RN, Columbia University; 7 years as school nurse

Counselors: 22
Men 5% Women 95% Min. age 18
Ratio to campers 1: 4

Health and safety:
Infirmary, RN on staff; doctor on call; hospital nearby

Concentration:
Trips and camping, drama, dance, arts and crafts, woodworking, hiking, tennis, swimming, sailing, canoeing, boating

Mission:
"Onaway provides each girl the time and space to develop the physical and spiritual strength necessary to meet the challenges of today's world with honesty, courage and sensitivity."

This is a small girls' camp situated on seven-mile-long Newfound Lake, in central New Hampshire, and as pleasant a place as you're likely to find. The long shoreline is a white, sandy beach, the lake water is crystal-clear, and tall white pines tower over this old campus. Buildings are a rustic dark brown, ornamented with snow-white trim, and connect to one another by worn, pine-needled paths. Everywhere you go, the campus is natural, yet perfectly neat and tidy. Educationally, this camp is just as carefully managed.

Each of Onaway's campers lives in a tiny, screened-in cabin with only one other girl her own age. Over the seven weeks, the cabin is their home to share, to decorate, and to keep clean. More challenging is that they must learn the give and take of getting along together—and the people here see that they do. The cabins are arranged in small clusters, of which there are seven, grouped by campers' ages. A bathroom and shower house is close to each group.

At Onaway the emphasis is on independence, leadership, self-motivation, decision making, spirituality, and the development of personal skills. Girls are divided into activity groups by age, and skill activities are further grouped according to ability. Campers may choose from a broad range of activities, both creative and athletic. Emphasis is always steered away from competition and toward each girl's individual growth as she learns to challenge herself.

All campers receive sailing instruction and take swimming six days a week, aiming for endurance. Other activities include tennis, arts and crafts, woodworking, sewing, environmental studies, creative writing, ceramics, classical dancing, boating, canoeing, sailing, nature study, campcraft, drama, field trips, sketching, games, photography, and choir.

Evenings at Onaway are relaxing times given to singing or entertainment, or maybe an evening canoe paddle or a quiet group reading. Sundays are quiet days. The choir sings at the service in the Hebron Community Church, and all campers dress in white for the five o'clock evening service at the outdoor chapel, followed by a cookout and then singing.

Trips go out of Onaway on a regular basis. Overnight camping trips go to such places as Baker River, Squam Lake (where *On Golden Pond* was filmed), and Mayhew Island. Cabin groups take turns spending overnights in remote lakeside lean-tos and cooking their meals over a campfire. Three levels of hiking clubs also go on three- to five-day trips into the nearby Presidential Range of the White Mountains, where they sleep in Appalachian Mountain Club huts. Overnight canoe trips explore different lakes and rivers of the White Mountains, and advanced canoeists are taken on a special white-water trip to Lake Umbagog and down the Androscoggin River. Fifteen- and sixteen-year-old girls can return to Onaway in the OWLE program (Onaway Wilderness Leadership Experience), in which they spend four and a half weeks canoeing, kayaking, and backpacking.

Meals at Onaway are superb. The dining room is a recently built hexagon, generously fitted with glass and screen, making the atmosphere bright, light, and airy. Campers sit on benches at tables and are served family-style from a delicious array of wholesome foods. Bread is baked daily by the chef; fresh fruit is available at every meal, and dinners are always accompanied by a fresh salad bar. In the center of the dining hall is a huge stone fireplace bearing a plaque that is dedicated to the previous director. The inscription reads: "God is in the song of a bird, in the beauty of a sunset, in a rushing brook, in the light of a star, and in you."

Camp Onaway is a place with definite ideals in mind: honor, justice, enthusiasm, cooperation. The standards set become habit-forming, things like cabin cleanup and wearing presentable uniforms. Each Sunday a cabin group presents a special program for the camp, maintaining a spiritual bond that is nourished daily by the saying of grace at meals, thought-for-the-day meetings, or quiet path talks.

This is one of those camps where campers and counselors vote with their feet. Between 65 and 75 percent return every year, the result of carefully planned, shared experiences as well as the fact that these girls are proud of themselves, both as individuals and as members of their community. At the end of the day, in an unaffected manner, the campers all gather together and link up in an unbroken chain that they call their "Closing Circle." It is a fitting symbol for the unity that exists between these girls tonight and which will no doubt endure for many of them long after their camping days are through.

Camp Osoha

Summer address:
11019 Big Muskellunge Lake Road
Boulder Junction, Wisconsin 15451

Phone:
(715) 385-2760

Winter address:
840 Tower Road
Winnetka, IL 60093

Phone:
(708) 441-6547

Natural features:
Secluded, naturally wooded, 13 acres with 1,000 feet of lake frontage in the middle of the Northern Highland State Forest

Nearest large city or town:
Minocqua

Enrollment:
Girls

Age spread:
8–16

Per summer:
75

Campers come from the:
East 9% Central 62% Southwest 4% Northwest 5% International 20%

Average number of international campers:
22—Mexico 15

Season:
June 21–August 9

Session (by percentage of campers) and cost:
4 weeks, 20%, $2,150
7 weeks, 80%, $3,300

Extra charges:
Some (riding $300–350; waterskiing $15–$25)

Financial structure:
For profit

Founded:
1921

Owner(s) and years associated with camp:
Linda Porter, 32

Manager(s) and years associated with camp:
Linda Porter, 32

Managing Director(s) and years associated with camp:
Linda Porter, 32

Other Director(s) and years associated with camp:
Ruth G. Weston, 29
Robin Reichl, 27

Director's background:
Linda Porter: B.S., physical education, Valparaiso University; M.Ed., specializing in guidance and counseling; 2½ years elementary school teacher; 8 years high school guidance; 3 years high school dean; 6 years camp counselor; 21 years camp director

Counselors: 25
Men 12% Women 88% Min. age 18
Ratio to campers 1: 3

Health and safety:
Infirmary, RN on staff; clinic nearby

Concentration:
Waterfront activities and tripping, based on camper's individual schedule

Mission:
"To be the best of whatever you are. To build up radiant health, to teach the joy of outdoor sports, to develop initiative, dependability, resourcefulness and individuality, and to cultivate the art of living with others."

Osoha sits on the northwest shore of Big Muskellunge Lake in northern Wisconsin, a secluded, wooded spot in the middle of the 210,000-acre Northern Highland State Forest. The campus occupies thirteen acres, with a thousand feet of lake frontage, and is three miles from the nearest highway.

Remote as it is, Osoha's stone-pillared entrance is a welcomed sight. As you stroll the earthen paths from log cabin to log cabin, it's not long before you fall under the spell of this pastoral setting. The entire campus is neat and carefully planned while still managing to hold on to its rustic quality.

Facilities are top-notch throughout. The lodge, only a few feet from the lake, contains an extensive library, a piano, and a beautiful fireplace. The office and kitchen complex are also in this building. The dining room is contained inside a large screened porch with tables that seat eight to ten people, two of whom are counselors.

There are eight log cabins in which ten campers live with two or three counselors, but without plumbing or electricity. A bathhouse with hot and cold running water, showers, and flush toilets is available to everyone at camp. Each cabin provides a full, screened-in view of the lake and has a porch that runs the length of the cabin. A small pier leading from each cabin provides the girls with their own access to the lake for unscheduled (but always supervised) dips.

Osoha's facilities are first-rate. The waterfront consists of canoe racks and a landing area, with areas for sailing, windsurfing, and waterskiing, and a 270-foot-long wooden pier with a diving board and diving tower. The riding area incorporates a stable, corral, and wooded riding ring. Double badminton courts and a partial basketball court are also used for volleyball.

Osoha's program is both well conceived and carried out, with a view to providing optimum experiences for all the campers here. Once each girl has sampled all of the camp's offerings, she may select many of her activities, from which she will be placed in small instruction groups with other girls of similar skill, rather than by age or cabin.

Waterfront and trips programs are emphasized here; in particular, canoeing and wilderness (ecology) activities are strong. Girls may also learn swimming, lifesaving, diving, windsurfing, water ballet, canoeing, waterskiing, sailing, English riding, tennis, archery, badminton, dance, and music. In the arts and crafts program, pottery and needlepoint are specialized options.

The progression of weekly canoe trips ranges from the short around-the-lake excursions and day trips on nearby lakes and rivers, to four-day trips for the most experienced canoeists. Each camper may go on as many of these trips as her ability and stamina will allow. Hiking trips on the countless logging roads and nature trails in the North Woods take campers through a truly natural environment.

Special events include an operetta for campers ten years old and younger and an Olympics Day in which every camper participates in at least three events. The Fourth of July is celebrated by spending an afternoon at Crystal Lake, taking in a water-ski show, attending a barn dance at a neighboring camp, and finally watching a fireworks display. Each summer there are two water meets in which all campers participate in a wide variety of events, including war canoe races.

Getting acquainted is easy at Osoha. Girls are happy, polite, and genuinely nice to each other. Dining room seating is changed weekly to allow campers the chance to get to know everybody in camp. A sizable international population enhances the camp's mission of learning to live with others of differing backgrounds.

The people here live the values they teach. Every camper is known as a distinct, worthwhile individual by the staff and other campers alike. Each has her own distinct schedule tailor-made to her abilities, her personal goals, and her activity goals, and all are followed up on continually. This is a small, classy institution that knows precisely what it needs to do for its campers and does it with a lot of heart.

Pasquaney

Summer address:
HC 60, Box 1130
Bristol, New Hampshire 03222

Phone:
(603) 744-8043

Winter address:
5 South State Street
Concord, NH 03301

Phone:
(603) 225-4065

Natural features:
Located on 535 acres of hilly woodland along the eastern shore of Newfound Lake

Nearest large city or town:
Laconia, Plymouth, Bristol

Enrollment:
Boys

Age spread:
11–16

Per summer:
82

Campers come from the:
Northeast 51% Southeast 20% Central 8% Northwest 3% Southwest 7% International 11%

Average number of international campers:
9—Belgium 5, Switzerland 2

Season:
June 24–August 13

Session (by percentage of campers) and cost:
7 weeks, 100%, $3,350

Extra charges:
Very few (uniforms)

Scholarships:
20% of campers do not pay full tuition

Financial structure:
Private, not for profit

Founded:
1895

Owner(s) and years associated with camp:
Pasquaney Trust, 52

Managing Director(s) and years associated with camp:
John K. Gemmill, 41

Director's background:
John K. Gemmill: B.A., Hamilton College; M.A., Columbia University; teacher; Pasquaney camper, counselor, assistant director, director; former president, NH Camp Directors Association; former president, Audubon Society—NH; Chair, Trust for NH Lands

Counselors: 25
Men 100% Min. age 18
Ratio to campers 1: 3½

Health and safety:
Infirmary, doctor or RN on staff; hospital 10 minutes away

Concentration:
"We have the liberal arts approach to camping—variety."

Mission:
"Pasquaney hopes that through exposure to its sense of community, excellent council role
models, and formal and informal discussions about values that its campers will grow in self-
esteem and in concern for others and for the group as well as in ethical awareness."

Pasquaney is located on 535 acres of fields and hilly woodland on the eastern
shore of Newfound Lake, in central New Hampshire. The camp was founded
in 1895 by Edward S. Wilson, "to provide a healthful and natural life in the woods,
a life which will make boys strong, confident, self-reliant and efficient, able to do
and think for others as well as themselves."

Many things about Pasquaney are impressive, not the least of which is its continuity. Not only is this the oldest continuously operating summer camp for boys in
the United States, but in its ninety-eight years there have been only four directors,
and they have seen to it that Wilson's vision has remained intact.

The campus is picturesque. The main buildings—wonderful old structures—are
located about 1,500 feet up the hill from the water. Just below are five clay tennis
courts and a baseball field, while spread along the lake are the boathouse, bathhouse, swimming area, and picnic area. All the buildings and facilities are connected by quaint woodland trails.

A couple of buildings that bear mentioning are the two-thousand-volume
Rosemary Stanwood Memorial Library and the Watson Theater, a simple structure
absolutely brimming with tradition, its walls picturing every Pasquaney group from
1895 to the present. The theater is put to good use. Every Saturday night a group
of boys presents a production, and toward the end of the season campers present
three major dramatic productions, usually a melodrama, a light comedy, and a work
by Shakespeare, Molière, or Fielding.

Campers and nearly all counselors live in six connected dormitories. Meals are
prepared by a professional chef and served family-style, with eight campers and two
counselors at each table. Twice a week, campers enjoy evening picnics at the waterfront.

In its recruitment, Pasquaney has always aimed for diversity in its campers—

geographic, cultural, and economic. Such a varied group is the raw material with which these experienced people meld a close-knit community. That is precisely this camp's goal, and everything about Pasquaney is deliberate and aimed in that direction. The single seven-and-a-half-week session, for example, assures that the community that begins here will see the season through as a group. The camp uniform serves to symbolize this unity while negating any superficial advantages/disadvantages of styles.

This is a place where boys and young men have both the time and motivation to discuss values while they put them into practice. Campers take turns handling duties such as sweeping dormitories, setting tables, and caring for tennis courts, all of which teaches about contributing to one's community. Leadership is also stressed here with two honor societies, White Pine for younger boys and Sigma Alpha for older campers. Among the older boys, the most qualified leaders are elected by the council as "Captains of Industry."

Although boys are separated by age for activities, lots of activities cut across age groups, enabling younger boys to both associate with and learn from their big brothers. Boys may choose from baseball, canoeing, camping, crew, diving, hiking, music, natural history, sailing, shop (the woodworking program is particularly strong), swimming/life-saving, tennis, theater, and various water sports, including war canoe races, canoe tilts, obstacle races, and dinghy races. There are day-long hikes into the White Mountains, overnight camping expeditions, and a week-long hike for the older boys.

This camp has a deep reverence for tradition. Customary practices have been played out year in and year out for nearly a century, in the same place and by very similar people. The mission in all that time has been simply to do two things: (1) make sure that each camper who leaves here has a better sense of himself, his own self-worth, and how he can be his best; and (2) see that each camper understands his opportunities and obligations to, first, become a member of a close-knit community where he will make deep and lasting friendships, and, later, be a contributor to whatever community he may find himself in.

Red Arrow Camp for Boys

Summer address:
3980 Day Lake Road
Woodruff, Wisconsin 54568

Phone or Fax:
(715) 385-2769

Winter address:
P.O. Box 881755
Steamboat Springs, CO 80477-1755

Phone or Fax:
(303) 879-7081

Natural features:
Situated on Trout Lake, bordered on one side by the Trout River; 1600-foot elevation

Nearest large city or town:
Rhinelander

Enrollment:
Boys

Age spread:
7½–16

Per summer:
100

Campers come from the:
Northeast 9% Southeast 7% Central 50%
Northwest 2% Southwest 9% International 23%

Average number of international campers:
23—Mexico 20, France 2

Season:
Third week in June to second week in August

Session (by percentage of campers) and cost:
7 weeks, 100%, $3,000

Extra charges:
Some (horseback riding, senior trips, skeet shooting)

Scholarships:
8–10% of campers do not pay full tuition

Financial structure:
For profit

Founded:
1920

Owner(s) and years associated with camp:
Bob and Sue Krohn, 29

Managing Director(s) and years associated with camp:
Bob and Sue Krohn, 29

Other Director(s) and years associated with camp:
Fred Albright, 27

Directors' backgrounds:
Bob Krohn: B.S., M.A. education, Northwestern University; 32 years coaching and teaching at high school and university levels; over 32 years in camping

Sue Krohn: B.S., M.A. education, University of Wisconsin; elementary school teacher; waterfront director; camp director

Fred Albright: B.S., M.A. education, University of Wisconsin; Ph.D. psychology and counseling, Stanford; 20 years teaching, counseling, coaching at high school and university levels

Counselors: 24
Men 100% Min. age 19
Ratio to campers 1: 3½

Health and safety:
Infirmary, RN on staff; hospital 10 miles away

Concentration:
"We do not focus on one specialty—we focus on all specialties! Our most popular activities are waterskiing, tennis, riflery, horseback riding, soccer and woodworking shop. We spend a great deal of time on tripping."

Mission:
"Friendship, self-confidence, self-worth, self-esteem, development and improvement of skills in various activities of camper's interests, development of social skills through cabin life and group living, development of outdoor skills and appreciation of woods, water, land and animals through respect for and ongoing improvement of environment, and to have FUN while doing any and all of the above!"

If there were a model of just what a boys' camp ought to be, Red Arrow Camp might be it. Located on the shore of Trout Lake, in northern Wisconsin's canoe country, and bounded on another side by the Trout River, Red Arrow has operated continuously for over seventy years on land (and in buildings) that once served as a nineteenth-century lumbering company and was well known as Indian camping grounds long before that.

Many of the 1850-vintage log cabins are not only still being used, but they're in absolutely mint condition, carefully chinked each year and well on their way into another century. Playing fields, courts, and grounds are likewise kept in splendid shape, shaded by tall white pines and Norway spruces. The lake is crystal-clear; the shore, twelve hundred feet of sandy, gradually deepening beach. This is land at its very best, serving a wonderful camp that celebrates putting the most into everything you do. A huge sign at the camp's entrance proclaims: *"Yes I can!"*

Red Arrow is run by directors who are superb role models not only for the campers but for the staff as well. Bob and Sue Krohn live their conviction by working right in the trenches, where they get to know every one of their campers. Both of them teach daily as well as administer the overall program. This is clearly an educational institution run by educators who know and love people and whose

considerable influence rubs off. The leadership at all levels is experienced, dedicated, and convinced of the importance of their work.

Where most camps offer different-length sessions to maximize enrollment, Red
Arrow does not waver from its single seven-week session, and its enrollment never
suffers. The camp enjoys good geographical diversity, with boys from a wide range
of states and countries.

Boys are separated into three age groups: Cubs (7–11$\frac{1}{2}$), Midgets (11$\frac{1}{2}$–13$\frac{1}{2}$),
and Seniors (13$\frac{1}{2}$–16). From eight to twelve campers live with two counselors in
each of eleven old log cabins, which are equipped with electric lights, screen windows, and double bunks.

Red Arrow's activities program is centered on instruction, with staff members
who are frequently upgrading their own skills. These people strive to separate
competition from instruction. It may be like splitting hairs in some cases—say, in
softball or basketball—but they are generally successful, and that tells a lot about the
fine overseeing of the program.

After an initial day's introduction to all of Red Arrow's offerings, campers
select seven activities (plus swimming, which is mandatory) that will be taught on
an every-other-day basis (four per day). At the end of two weeks and again after
three weeks, there are sign-up days in which boys are encouraged to change at least
one of their activities.

Activities include wrestling, flag football, track, soccer, softball, basketball,
swimming, skin diving, scuba diving, sailing, windsurfing, waterskiing, photography, photo processing, choir, dramatics, stagecraft, weight training, physical fitness,
nature/ecology, trapshooting, archery, riflery, tennis, horseback riding, wood shop,
and a wonderful fifteen-element ropes course, complete with a three-hundred-foot
zip line. There are also opportunities for campers to participate in other activities
during morning and afternoon general times. For campers who wish to be on a
team, Red Arrow teams compete with neighboring camps in softball, basketball,
soccer, track, tennis, swimming, and riflery, with teams in each age group.

Red Arrow outfits campers for at least two cabin trips a summer, by raft, canoe,
backpack, and bicycle. Trippers go into the Porcupine Mountains or as far away as
northern Ontario for canoeing, fishing, and exploring.

The camp dining room is a spacious log building over 140 years old, neat as can
be, with paddles hanging on the log walls from each year the camp has been in
existence. The campers assist in menu planning, and the food is fine and nutritious.
There is fresh fruit at dinner and either ice cream or a baked dessert daily; but

there's no candy or soda allowed here, except at Thursday night's songfest, when boys are each given one bottle of soda.

The Red Arrow staff enjoys an impressive 75 to 80 percent return rate each year. Not surprisingly, most counselors (all but one) are former Red Arrow campers. Ninety percent are either college undergraduates or schoolteachers. In every activity, every day, this camp attempts to help its campers to both feel better about themselves and find more successful ways to get along with others.

Red Pine Camp for Girls

RED PINE CAMP FOR GIRLS

Address:
Box 69
Minocqua, Wisconsin 54548

Phone:
(715) 356-6231
Fax (715) 356-1077

Natural features:
The only privately owned property on Clear Lake

Nearest large city or town:
Rhinelander (airport)

Enrollment:
Girls

Age spread:
6–16

Per summer:
100

Campers come from the:
Northeast 5% Central 50% Southeast 5%
Northwest 5% Southwest 5% International 30%

Average number of international campers:
30—Mexico 8, Venezuela 2, Brazil, England, France, Spain

Season:
June 21–August 14

Session (by percentage of campers) and cost:
4 weeks, 65%, $1,665
8 weeks, 35%, $3,280

Extra charges:
Some (riding fees $275–450)

Financial structure:
For profit

Founded:
1938

Owner(s) and years associated with camp:
Helen and Richard Wittenkamp, 57 (founders)

Managing Director(s) and years associated with camp:
Sarah Wittenkamp Rolley, life

Director's background:
Sarah Wittenkamp Rolley: B.A., psychology, University of Kansas; daughter of founders, on camp staff since 1953; 25-year member, ACA

Counselors: 36
Men 5% Women 95% Min. age 19
Ratio to campers 1: 3

Health and safety:
Infirmary, 4 RNs on staff; hospital 4 miles away

Concentration:
Waterfront, riding, arts, and tennis are among the many activities offered; the camp stresses safety

Mission:

"Self-competitive. To live and perform to the best of one's ability, with consideration of others at all times. An individual award is presented to each camper in recognition of her outstanding ability, trait of character or personality."

Tucked away on Clear Lake, in northern Wisconsin, this is as charming a campus as you're likely to find. Buildings are ornamented with flowers. Playing fields, courts, and waterfront are all fastidiously cared for. And 1,200-acre Clear Lake is most aptly named, a lovely spring-fed body of water with only one private property on its shores—Red Pine.

Over the years, the Wittenkamp family (in its second generation of operating Red Pine) has attended this property with loving care to every detail. For example, power lines are buried underground, allowing for all the buildings to be equipped with modern conveniences without the sight of overhead wires or utility poles. And it seems that everywhere you walk through the white birch and pine trees there are freshly painted little signs to guide you along the hilly terrain.

An attractive waterfront lodge serves as an all-around recreation facility for the camp, whether as a cool retreat during the day or a place for music practice or drama rehearsals on its fine stage. At night, the lodge is a firelit gathering place for songs and skits, a warm camp environment whose walls are decorated with flags representing the countries of each of the campers and a handmade quilt commemorating the founders' sixtieth wedding anniversary.

Campers are grouped into four cabin units based on age, grade, skills, emotional and physical requirements, special interests, and previous camping experience. The youngest of them reside in the Starlet Unit, consisting of three cabins and a staff-to-camper ratio of 1:3. Junior campers stay in the Forester Unit, which has four cabins and the same staff-to-camper ratio. Teenagers are assigned to the Ranger Unit high on a hill overlooking the lake, with a staff-to-camper ratio of 1:5. The oldest campers are part of the Pioneer Unit, which resides in three cabins on a woodsy ridge and whose staff-to-camper ratio is 1:7. All cabins have lake views, and all are electrically lighted and equipped with modern sanitary facilities.

Campers and their counselors dine together as cabin groups in a dining room that is clean and sunny, with a wide porch overlooking the lake. On warm days campers eat outdoors, sometimes on lake pontoons.

Red Pine's program is free-choice and self-competitive. A camper's pursuit of her individual goals is what is always encouraged. In fact, she may even schedule double periods for herself so that she can spend twice as long on a favorite activity.

Red Pine offers aerobics, aerobic jazz, archery, arts and crafts, basketball, camp-craft, canoeing, cheerleading, dancing, dramatics, first aid, free swims, English rid-ing, sailing, swimming (Red Cross, competitive, and synchronized), tae kwon do, tennis, overnight tripping, tutoring (upon request), volleyball, water aerobics, and windsurfing. Near the end of the session, accomplished older campers are selected for an eight-day honor trip, usually into Canadian or boundary waters.

Red Pine's program is considerably enhanced by the fact that each counselor is a specialist in his or her activity field. Many of the young women are former Red Pine campers who have gone through Red Pine's Leadership Training, a three-year program offered to outstanding campers from the Pioneer Unit.

There are several different awards available as recognition of a camper's ability or character trait. And there are always plenty of special events and activities—things like intercamp regattas and tennis matches, a water-sports day, piñata party, song contests, or Little Sister–Big Sister Days.

Continuity is the word that best describes this camp. Whether it's the excellent cook, who is in her fifteenth year with the camp, or the fact that the camp has remained in the same family since its founding (and will likely pass on to a third generation), campers who come to Red Pine are living, eating, and breathing tradition in one of the most pleasant summer environments there could be.

Rockbrook Camp

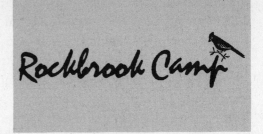

Address:
P.O. Box 792
Brevard, North Carolina 28712

Phone:
(704) 884-6151

Natural features:
Located on a mountainside at 2,250 feet elevation; wooded terrain with streams; surrounded by mountain range.

Nearest large city or town:
Between Greenville, SC, and Asheville, NC

Enrollment:
Girls

Age spread:
6–15

Per summer:
579

Campers come from the:
Southeast 89% Northeast 5% Central 2% Northwest 1% Southwest 1% International 2%

Average number of international campers:
12—Colombia 2, France 2, Germany 2, Japan 2, Mexico 2, Venezuela 2

Season:
Second week in June to second week in August

Session (by percentage of campers) and cost:
2 weeks, 30%, $995
3$\frac{1}{2}$ weeks, 70%, $1,595

Extra charges:
Incidentals only

Financial structure:
For profit

Founded:
1921

Owner(s) and years associated with camp:
Jerry Stone, 29

Managing Director(s) and years associated with camp:
Jerry Stone, 29

Other Director(s) and years associated with camp:
Jan Gillean, 17

Directors' backgrounds:
Jerry Stone: 11 years college administrator; involved in outdoor education since 1961

Jan Gillean: M.Ed.; college administrator

Counselors: 70
Women 100% Min. age 18
Ratio to campers 1: 2$\frac{1}{2}$

Health and safety:
Infirmary, RNs on staff; hospital nearby

Concentration:
Free-choice program of 20 activities; noteworthy are outdoor programs (white-water rafting, canoeing, rock climbing, backpacking and mountain biking), gymnastics, tennis, riding (hunt seat), pottery, drama

Mission

"To participate in a child's growing up and to make a significant contribution to their feeling good about themselves. The camp program and environment is designed to provide many opportunities for fostering self-reliance. This is accomplished by providing positive role models on the staff who teach them in a non-competitive environment."

Rockbrook is an old, well-respected girls' camp situated in the lush, green, mountainous countryside of southwestern North Carolina. Given a setting such as this, with a lake, a brook that meanders all through the campus, many first-rate facilities, and a sound educational philosophy, this place is hard to beat.

Rockbrook girls are grouped into three age units—Juniors, Middlers, and Seniors—who sleep in rustic cabins, all of which offer commanding views of the surrounding valley and mountains beyond. Two counselors, or a counselor and a counselor assistant, live in the cabins with the girls. Each cabin group has its own stone lodge (with fireplace) and bathhouse with hot showers.

Each unit also has its own program of activities, administered in terms of age, ability, and interest of the camper. Within the unit's program, a camper may choose among various activities that challenge her according to her own pace and strengths. Rockbrook's program is based on a noncompetitive philosophy that emphasizes activities like climbing and outdoor adventure—not surprising since the camp's director is a former U.S. Army Ranger.

Sports training for all ages includes gymnastics and other gym sports, tennis (all campers are encouraged to participate in the tennis program), archery, riflery, and other land sports. Horseback riding is an important feature at Rockbrook, too. Facilities include riding rings, a variety of jumps, and two hunt courses enclosed in the pastures. Horse shows are held at the end of the sessions.

The swimming program is designed for safety, with campers classified according to American Red Cross specifications. Synchronized swimming, water ballet, basic rescue, and advanced lifesaving are offered, along with two free swims per day.

Canoeing instruction is geared to river canoeing. After girls learn basic skills in the camp lake, they are taken on short trips to easy rivers, gradually working their way up to the challenges of some of the nearby mountain rivers such as the Green, the Chattooga, the Tuckasiegee, and the Nantahala, which boasts one of the most famous sections of white water in the East. To enhance this fine program, Rockbrook owns a Nantahala outpost, which serves the advanced whitewater instruction.

Rock climbing has been an integral part of Rockbrook's program for older campers since 1976. Beginners learn on the climbing wall inside the camp gymnasium, while more advanced climbers practice on some of the in-camp rock faces. As a girl advances, she progresses to out-of-camp climbs in and around Pisgah National Forest. Rockbrook also offers its older girls a top-notch high ropes course to boost confidence, as well as other activities such as night hikes, mountain biking, and white-water activities.

A good deal of attention is paid to creative endeavors here, such as the publication of the *Carrier Pigeon*, Rockbrook's camp book that comes out at the end of each season. The pottery studio is the centerpiece of the crafts program, housing a resident potter who devotes full time to instructing campers in the summer, while using camp facilities in the off-season to create and sell his own pottery. Weaving, basketry, needlecrafts, dancing, and drama are also important components of the arts and crafts program.

Rockbrook is an institution that knows what it is and where it's going. It is a comfortable place, quiet and serene; serious, but with a sense of humor. Here girls are exposed to real wilderness adventures, with other girls and leaders who continually boost their confidence by showing them that there is no limit to what they can accomplish. It's a camp with real soul, an ideal place for a girl to retreat, to make friends, to be challenged, to play, and mostly to grow.

Sanborn Western Camps

Big Spring Ranch for Boys
High Trails Ranch for Girls

Address:
P.O. Box 167
Florissant, Colorado 80816

Phone:
(719) 748-3341

Natural features:
6,000 acres of mountain meadow and forest at an elevation of 8,700 feet; adjacent to national forest and national park

Nearest large city or town:
Colorado Springs

Enrollment:
Coed
Boys 50% Girls 50%

Age spread:
8–17

Per summer:
600

Campers come from the:
Northeast 18% Southeast 4% Central 62%
Northwest 4% Southwest 4% International 8%

Average number of international campers:
47—France 12, Sweden 10, England 5, Germany 5, Japan 4, Mexico 4, Switzerland 4, Italy 3

Season:
June 16–August 23

Session (by percentage of campers) and cost:
5 weeks, 100% (2 sessions), $2,350

Extra charges:
None

Financial structure:
For profit

Founded:
1948

Owner(s) and years associated with camp:
Sanborn family, 46

Managing Director(s) and years associated with camp:
Rick Sanborn, 42
Jane Sanborn, 25

Other Director(s) and years associated with camp:
Roger Sanborn, 46
Laura Sanborn, 46

Directors' backgrounds:
Rick Sanborn: B.S., botany, Colorado State University

Jane Sanborn: B.A., English/education, Colorado College

Roger Sanborn: B.S., Colorado State University

Laura Sanborn: B.A., Colorado State University

Counselors: 70
Men 50% Women 50% Min. age 20
Ratio to campers 1: 5

Health and safety:
Infirmaries, 4 RNs on staff; doctors on call;
hospital nearby

Concentration:
Backpacking and mountaineering, western riding, nature, geology, astronomy, tripping; also: sports, waterfront activities, arts and crafts

Mission:
"To provide an exciting, safe and rewarding experience in the out-of-doors in which everyone: gains in self-confidence, independence and the ability to live with others; develops a greater feeling for the beauty of the Earth and uses their senses to feel alive and part of the Earth—not apart from it; learns new skills and improves old ones, lives each day to its fullest, using increased understanding to learn to live together and work towards a better world."

You know even before you set foot in this camp where its heart is. Flags representing each foreign camper's country—and there are many—are flown every hundred yards along the long entrance. Sanborn is a place with a world view of harmony. The land is pristine, 8,500 feet high, and graced everywhere with wildflowers, tall pines, rocky bluffs, and tremendous views of snow-capped peaks in the distance. The air feels healthy and clean, and after a while you understand that the staff are doing everything they can to make sure it stays that way. The examples they set for their campers, both subtle and not so, are numerous. For instance, each building has its own simple but carefully kept flower garden. And all over the campus, trails are carefully laid for specific purposes, whether for fitness or ecology or even star-gazing.

Sanborn is aptly advertised as a "Five-Week Adventure in Learning." Unquestionably, this is an educational institution, and one whose method is steeped in high adventure and diversity. And the Sanborns see to it that the program remains gender-blind. Even though the boys' and girls' camps are separated by a half-mile, there is no difference in their programs. Girls do what boys do, and boys do what girls do.

With assistance from counselors and program leaders, each camper selects an individualized program of activities from the twelve to sixteen options offered daily.

Although backpacking and mountaineering are understandably emphasized in this environment (at this elevation, there are no poisonous snakes, poison ivy, poison oak, or other similar natural hazards), many other unique opportunities abound.

The western riding program offers breakfast and sunset rides, branding, cattle roundup, gymkhana, and many more activities. Over 100 camp-owned horses are kept at Sanborn year-round, and every rider can go out on one- to five-night pack trips to one of Sanborn's back-country outpost camps and other locations, including the South Platte River Canyon and wilderness areas of South Park. Advanced riders may sign on to help with the chores of a working cattle ranch.

In the nature program there's fossil and crystal digging, gold panning, solar experiments, pond-life searches, sensory-awareness activities, and something called "Mad Scientists." Astronomy is a featured program at Sanborn, offering telescopic viewing, planetarium shows, and astronomy overnights.

Sports include tennis, archery, basketball, volleyball, softball, lacrosse, soccer, tumbling, and more, as well as many games that may be new to many campers, like schmeritz, yoshi, spud, earthball, and steal the bacon. Water sports include fishing, swimming, diving, synchronized swimming, rafting, canoeing, tubing, and water polo.

Several creative arts and crafts are offered, such as drama, modern dance, camp newspaper, photography, lapidary, pottery, leather and metal work, fly-tying, and more.

Western history includes ghost-town explorations, arrowhead searches, blacksmithing, etc. And there are always special events, from traditional campfire songs and stories to treehouse sleep-outs, casino night, silent trails, talent night, and lots more.

In the hiking/mountaineering program there are many activities, from high mountain backpacks and overnights to lone vigils and prospecting overnights. The hiking program progresses from day-long adventure trips to five-day trips into the high mountain peaks and alpine valleys along the Continental Divide. Camp-owned property at 11,000 feet in Horseshoe Valley serves as a mountain base camp for alpine explorations and the Mount Sherman climb. Older campers may choose to participate in technical rock climbing, taught by specialists in the rock climbing school.

Each of the Sanborn camps has a heated swimming pool, tennis courts, theater building, crafts building, dining room, infirmary, stables, barn, riding area, and fine sports areas. The camps share the Interbarn/Interpretive Center as well as several learning centers around the ranch, including an Indian Tipi Village, an 1890s Pioneering Homestead, the Witcher Cattle Ranch, a Solar Hut, 1900 Sawmill, several geology sites, and the Astronomy Pad.

This is an extraordinary institution, not only warm and nurturing but extremely well managed. The Sanborns have a deep family tradition as educators, and they are as ambitious and conscientious as any camp directors I have seen. They are really trying to make a difference in the world, and they are succeeding.

Camp Sea Gull
(For Boys)

Camp Seafarer
(For Girls)

Summer address:
Camp Sea Gull
Rt. 65, Box 1
Arapahoe, North Carolina 28510

Camp Seafarer
Rt. 65, Box 3
Arapahoe, North Carolina 28510

Phone:
Sea Gull: (919) 249-1111
Seafarer: (919) 249-1212

Winter address:
Camp Sea Gull
P.O. Box 10976
Raleigh, NC 27605

Camp Seafarer
Rt. 65, Box 3
Arapahoe, NC 28510

Phone:
Sea Gull: (919) 832-6601
Seafarer: (919) 249-1212

Natural features:
350 acres of grounds situated on the 5-mile-wide coastal Neuse River

Nearest large city or town:
New Bern

Enrollment:
Sea Gull: boys
Seafarer: girls

Age spread:
7–16

Per summer:
Sea Gull: 1,520
Seafarer: 1,132

Campers come from the:
Northeast 7% Southeast 65% Mid Atlantic 15% Central 8% Northwest 1% Southwest 3% International 2%

Average number of international campers:
23—France 3, Spain 3, Venezuela 3, Germany 2, Mexico 2

Season:
June 4–August 11

Session (by percentage of campers) and cost:
4 weeks, 85% (2 sessions), $1,750
1 week, 15%, $400

Extra charges:
Some (long cruise $140, horseback riding $160)

Financial structure:
Agency-owned, not for profit

Founded:
Sea Gull: 1948
Seafarer: 1961

Owner(s) and years associated with camp:
Capitol Area YMCA of Raleigh, NC, 45

Managing Director(s) and years associated with camp:
Sea Gull:
Lloyd Griffith, 18

Seafarer:
Cille Griffith, 20

Other Director(s) and years associated with camp:
Sea Gull:
Bo Roberts, 20
Henry DeHart, 2
Rich Brown, 3

Seafarer:
Olivia Holding, 3
Bobby Harris, 9
Patricia Suggs, 3

Directors' backgrounds:
Sea Gull:
Lloyd Griffith: Master's in counseling; AB, Duke University, M. Div., Duke Divinity School; M.A. psychology, Lesley College

Bo Roberts: graduate, University of North Carolina

Rich Brown: B.S. business, East Carolina University

Henry DeHart: B.A. philosophy, Emery University

Seafarer:
Cille Griffith: B.A. in early childhood education; Meredith College; M.Ed., language arts, Framingham State University, camper, counselor, teacher, supervisor, consultant

Patricia Suggs: B.A. English, University of North Carolina

Olivia Holding: B.S. political science, University of North Carolina; M.A. education, George Washington University

Bobby Harris: recreation degree, North Carolina State University

Counselors:
Sea Gull: 280
Men 95% Women 5% Min. age 17
Ratio to campers 1: 3

Seafarer: 195
Men 5% Women 95% Min. age 18
Ratio to campers 1: 3

Health and safety:
Sea Gull:
Infirmary, 8 RNs/graduate nurses, 4 physicians on staff

Seafarer:
Infirmary, 7 RNs/graduate nurses, 2 physicians on staff

Concentration:
Sea Gull:
Seamanship program; golf, tennis, and other land activities

Seafarer:
Sailing and motorboating skills, plus riding, golf, tennis, and other land activities

Mission:
"Following the mission of the YMCA: to enrich the spiritual, mental, physical and social life of each person, to develop self-confidence, self-respect and an appreciation of campers' own worth as individuals, to grow as responsible members of their cabin and citizens of their communities,

to develop an appreciation of nature and God's outdoors, to develop and increase skills in a wide range of land, sea and special activities, and to develop an understanding of the worth of all individuals and the importance of teamwork."

Seagull and Seafarer are, as their names might suggest, camps with an emphasis on ocean activities, namely sailing. Situated seven miles apart (three miles by water), both camps are legendary in the southeastern United States because they are so well run in every aspect. Physically, these are beautiful campuses with magnificent facilities. Educationally, they are practically flawless. It's plain to see that great care and thought have gone into building and sustaining them.

Camp Seagull reminds me of a Hollywood depiction of what a seaside sailing camp on the North Carolina coast should look like. You go through a gate decorated with flower boxes and are greeted by a huge white ship's anchor and a carved sign bearing the camp name. The campus spreads out before you: a number of simple, spotless buildings set off by a series of immaculate lawns across which administrators are making their rounds on golf carts. Ten hard-surface tennis courts are set in the middle of the campus, all in excellent condition; just beyond lies the camp's professionally built eighteen-hole golf course, while down at the shore sailboats by the dozens decorate the water.

Both campuses are alike in their excellence, each with 350 acres of grounds, sturdy cabins, and first-rate facilities, including fresh-water swimming areas. Camp Sea Gull, in addition to its championship golf course and tennis courts, has a 1,000-foot pier and high and low ropes challenge courses. Camp Seafarer has eight tennis courts, a twenty-two-horse stable, a nine-hole pitch and putt golf course and driving range, full marina, a low ropes course, and a 750-foot pier.

Although such facilities provide for a land program that is every bit as good as any mentioned in this book, both Sea Gull and Seafarer concentrate on their seamanship programs. Supported by an outstanding fleet of sailboats, sailboards, power boats, outboards, and cruisers, the camps offer daily regattas and instruction in navigation as well as in sail, boat, and engine maintenance and repair. Proficiency in swimming is given highest priority at these camps, so all campers take swimming instruction daily. Long overnight cruises and deep-sea fishing trips are optional activities, as are waterskiing, fishing, and crabbing.

Camp Sea Gull's land activities include many athletics such as baseball, basketball, and soccer, as well as archery, tennis, riflery, canoeing, zip line, jeep trips, nature studies, arts and crafts, and an excellent golf program. Evening programs include usual camp activities as well as weekly dances for older campers.

Camp Seafarer's land program offers archery, golf, basketball, lacrosse, soccer, canoeing, riflery, tennis, arts and crafts, nature studies, and, for campers ten and older, a first-rate program of horseback riding. In both camps a Staff Trainee Program is available for qualified campers, fifteen and sixteen years old. Meals are served family-style in spacious, restaurant-clean dining rooms, and the kitchen facilities and staff of both camps are the best I've seen of any camp in my travels.

Because of the size of the camps, their age, and the tremendous support of the YMCA, the facilities and equipment are simply without parallel. Sea Gull and Seafarer will both endure for a long, long time. The counselors at both camps are professional, patient, and sincere, and their instruction is excellent. Children who come here know that they have gotten a first-rate experience.

On the Seafarer campus stands a memorial building named Taylor Lodge. It is dedicated to Wyatt and Lil Taylor, who founded this camp forty-four years ago with a singular philosophy that today remains solidly at the heart of both these camps: "Things don't just happen. You make them happen."

Camp Stewart for Boys

Heart O'the Hills Camp for Girls

Address:
Camp Stewart
Rt. 1, Box 110
Hunt, Texas 78024-9714

Heart O'the Hills
Hunt, Texas 78024-9720

Phone:
Camp Stewart: (210) 238-4670;
Fax (210) 238-4737
Heart O'the Hills: (210) 238-4650
Fax (210) 238-4737

Natural features:
Camp Stewart: situated on the headwaters of the Guadalupe River in the heart of Texas Hill Country, at 2,000 feet elevation; large playgrounds and rough back country

Heart O'the Hills: situated on the south fork of the Guadalupe River in the heart of Texas Hill Country, at 1,800 feet elevation

Nearest large city or town:
Kerrville, San Antonio

Enrollment:
Camp Stewart: boys
Heart O'the Hills: girls

Age spread:
6–16

Per summer:
Camp Stewart: 750
Heart O'the Hills: 400

Campers come from the:
Camp Stewart:
Southeast 3% Central 2% Northwest 1%
Northeast 1% Southwest 81% International 12%

Heart O'the Hills:
Northeast 1% Southeast 2% Central 1%
Northwest 1% Southwest 83% International 12%

Average number of international campers:
Camp Stewart: 64—Mexico 45, Spain 4, Indonesia 3, Canada 2, Hong Kong 2

Heart O'the Hills: 30—Mexico 25, Spain 2

Season:
June 7–August 24

Session (by percentage of campers) and cost:
Camp Stewart:
2½ weeks, 24%, $1,395
4 weeks, 76%, $1,995

Heart O'the Hills:
2½ weeks, 22%, $1,395
4 weeks, 78%, $1,985

Scholarships:
5% of campers do not pay full tuition

Extra charges:
Some (crafts supplies, store deposit, uniforms —approximately $115)

Financial structure:
For profit

Founded:
Camp Stewart: 1923
Heart O'the Hills: 1953

Owner(s) and years associated with camps:
Ragsdale family, 28

Managing Director(s) and years associated with camps:
Si and Kathy Ragsdale, 28

Other Director(s) and years associated with camps:
Camp Stewart:
Silas B. (Jeeper) Ragsdale III, 23
Luke Neslage, 14
George Morgan, 10

Heart O'the Hills:
C. Jane Ragsdale, 20
Lara Richardson, 9
Jill Hackney, 11

Directors' backgrounds:
Silas B. (Si) Ragsdale, Jr., Director: B.A., economics, University of Texas at Austin; Chairman, National Camping Advisory Council; past president, Camp Association for Mutual Progress; past member, Texas Governor Youth Camping advisory council; former camper, counselor; owner since 1966

Kathy C. Ragsdale, Codirector: B.S., B.A., journalism, English, Texas Woman's University; director emeritus, Texas Hunter Jumper Association

Jeeper Ragsdale, Associate Director: Schreiner College, University de San Miguel; double-gold winner Olympic Festival in stadium jumping; international jumping competitor; former camper, counselor; di-

rector of horseback; CHA (master) certification

Luke Neslage, Director of Programs: senior, Latin American studies, Vanderbilt University; former camper, counselor

George Morgan, Senior Camp Director: Dallas Baptist College; former counselor

C. Jane Ragsdale, Director: B.A., B.S., journalism, Spanish, Texas Woman's University; vice president, Camp Association of Mutual Progress; former camper, counselor, program director; NRA rifle instructor; WSI trainer

Lara Richardson, Associate Director: B.A., communications, Washington State University; former camper, counselor, program director

Jill Hackney, Assistant Program Director: University of Texas at Austin; former camper, counselor

Counselors:
Camp Stewart: 52
Men 96% Women 4% Min. age 18
Ratio to campers 1: 4

Heart O'the Hills: 40
Men 1% Women 99% Min. age 19
Ratio to campers 1: 3½

Health and safety:
Infirmary, RN on staff; medical center 18 miles away

Concentration:
Camp Stewart:
English/western horseback; all field and gym sports; tennis, water sports, nature and wilderness camping, riflery, archery, music, ceramics

Heart O'the Hills:
swimming, horseback riding, field sports, art, and a variety of other activities

Mission:

Camp Stewart:

"Attention on the total development of the boy; to build self-confidence and a feeling of self-worth, along with the learning of new skills, making lasting friends and developing independence, all while having new experiences, all in the spirit of fun. Our Motto: 'Don't wait to be a man to be great—be a great boy!'"

Heart O'the Hills:

"We focus not just on tangible skills but on the intangibles: self-confidence, teamwork, leadership, individual identity, dealing with challenges. The Heart has long had a tradition of etiquette."

With hills of hardwood forests and well-groomed fields all around, a stately cypress- and pecan-lined river frames the setting of these fine brother and sister camps. Although the two camps are operated (and were founded) by the same family, they remain separate both in location and in their programs.

Camp Stewart's facilities are extraordinary, among the best anywhere, and the large number of boys who come here enables the camp to offer more than eighty activities. If a boy is interested in sports, he couldn't do much better than this place.

Start with six baseball diamonds and a regulation football field, all equipped with an underground sprinkler system, and you may begin to get the picture. Other facilities include a spacious gymnasium, seven tennis courts (three lighted), four soccer fields, a small golf course and large putting green, a 400-meter track, areas for long and broad jump, 100 horses (most registered with the American Quarter Horse Association), extensive waterfront (diving boards, twenty canoes, several kayaks, and playaks), NRA rifle range, archery range, campcraft area, nature museum, arts and crafts center, band and choral building, Green Cathedral for Sunday (Christian and nondenominational) services, infirmary, canteen, dining hall, two recreational halls, etc. In addition, well-known personalities from sports, arts, wildlife, business, and politics frequently visit to teach special clinics, making the already-excellent instruction one notch better.

One of Stewart's unique features is its advancement program, wherein campers thirteen and older may specialize in one of five fields: Outdoorsman (rappelling, survival camping, etc.), Sportsman (all activities plus conditioning), Ranchman (farm animals, Texas ranch life, etc.), Equestrian (hunt-seat riding, jumping polo-crosse, etc.), or Campmaster (traditional camp program), in addition to the regular activities.

Advancement in self-confidence and personal growth, not just in skills, is key at Stewart. As campers progress from year to year, they earn certain awards. For example, fifth-year campers go on an all-expense-paid trip to Monterey, Mexico.

Although Heart O'the Hills is not as large nor as sports-oriented as its brother camp, its facilities and activities program are impressive nonetheless, and its traditional values are a close match to Stewart's. Uniforms are worn, and manners and etiquette are stressed.

The campus is charming, an expanse of manicured lawns, stone buildings, and straight wooden fences. The camp centerpiece is a former luxurious resort inn built of rock and petrified wood. Fully air-conditioned, the lodge houses the camp dining room as well as the "tepees" (former hotel rooms) in which the younger (ages six to ten) campers live. Older campers (eleven and up) live in more traditional cabins (which are also air-conditioned).

"The Heart" offers forty to fifty activities each term, and campers may select up to ten of these to take on a regular basis. Each camper is asked to take field sports, swimming, and western riding, scheduled by age and expertise. Other activities include English riding, horsemanship, archery, riflery, tennis, golf, canoeing, diving, competitive swimming, pioneering, fishing, dance (ballet, jazz, tap), gymnastics, nature crafts, arts and crafts, calligraphy, leather work, textiles, needlework and painting, sign language, cheerleading, journalism, life skills, war canoe, and more. Field sports include track, basketball, volleyball, soccer, flag football, softball, flickerball, and pickleball.

The riding program is supported by a large, covered grandstand, two arenas, and thirty horses. Those campers desiring extra riding may take English riding or horsemanship. Beginning jumping is also offered. As at Stewart, this and other programs are bolstered by frequent clinics given by visiting specialists.

Heart O'the Hills has three waterfront areas and, through the Red Cross Swimming Program, instructs girls from beginning swimmer to advanced lifesaving. Synchronized swimming, diving, and competitive swimming are also taught as electives.

The Ragsdale family is totally committed to both of these camps. They create an affectionate, exciting, and often humorous atmosphere, all the while maintaining traditional values: simple uniforms, groomed and courteous counselors, and genuinely polite and obedient campers. These people—owners, staff, and campers alike—are unreservedly proud of their camps, with very good reason.

The Susquehannock Camps

Susquehannock for Boys
Susquehannock for Girls

Summer address:
Susquehannock for Boys
RD 1, Box 71
Brackney, Pennsylvania 18812

Susquehannock for Girls
Box 48
Friendsville, Pennsylvania 18818

Phone:
Susquehannock for Boys: (717) 967-2323
or (717) 663-2188; Fax (717) 967-2631
Susquehannock for Girls: (717) 553-2343

Winter address:
Susquehannock for Boys
RD 1, Box 71
Brackney, PA 18812

Susquehannock for Girls
860 Briarwood Road
Newtown Square, PA 19073

Phone:
Susquehannock for Boys: (717) 967-2323
or (717) 663-2188; Fax (717) 967-2631
Susquehannock for Girls: (215) 356-3426

Natural features:
Susquehannock for Boys: 1,200 acres surrounded by woodlands, including a 40-acre lake

Susquehannock for Girls: 750-acre campus with fields, forest, and private lake

Nearest large city or town:
Montrose, PA, or Binghamton, NY

Enrollment:
Separate camps for boys and girls

Age spread:
Susquehannock for Boys: 7–16
Susquehannock for Girls: 7–17

Per summer:
Susquehannock for Boys: 225
Susquehannock for Girls: 140

Campers come from the:
Susquehannock for Boys:
Northeast 75% Southeast 5% International 10%

Susquehannock for Girls:
Northeast 75% Southeast 7% International 18%

Average number of international campers:
Susquehannock for Boys:
Spain 6, France 5, Venezuela 5, Mexico 3

Susquehannock for Girls:
Venezuela 4, Austria 3, France 3, Spain 3, Italy 2

Season:
June 26–August 19

Session (by percentage of campers) and cost:
4 weeks, 65%, $1,950
6 weeks, 10%, $2,750
8 weeks, 25%, $3,500

Extra charges:
Some (tutoring; horseback riding—$200–$650, depending on extent)

Scholarships:
5% of campers do not pay full tuition

Financial structure:
For profit

Founded:
Susquehannock for Boys: 1905
Susquehannock for Girls: 1986

Owner(s) and years associated with camp:
Shafer family, 90

Managing Director(s) and years associated with camp:
Susquehannock for Boys:
Edwin H. Shafer, Jr., 21

Susquehannock for Girls:
Dede Shafer, 9
George Shafer, 9

Other Director(s) and years associated with camp:
Susquehannock for Boys:
George B. Weigand, 41
David Reeve, 22
Thomas D. Kent, 16
Anthony Meyers, 14
Enos Young, 31

Susquehannock for Girls:
Cannie C. Shafer, 12
G. Carlton Shafer III, 9

Directors' backgrounds:
Edwin H. Shafer, Jr.: B.A., University of Pennsylvania; faculty, Episcopal Academy; coach: golf, ice hockey, soccer official; 9 years Assistant Director

Louise H. (Dede) Shafer: Served on staff of Susquehannock for Boys for 40 years; former camper/counselor

George Shafer: A.B., Princeton University; M.A., Columbia University; teacher/coach, Episcopal Academy, 42 years; camper/counselor/director, Susquehannock Camps since age 6

Enos Young: B.S./M.A., Gettysburg College; high school physical education teacher; head coach, football; coach of basketball, baseball, tennis, and golf

Cannie C. Shafer: B.A., Sweet Briar College; M.A., Villanova University

G. Carlton Shafer III: B.A., The College of Wooster; major, U.S.M.C.R.

Counselors:
Susquehannock for Boys: 45
Men 90% Women 10% Min. age 18
Ratio to campers 1: $4^{1}/_{2}$

Susquehannock for Girls: 22
Women 100% Min. age 18
Ratio to campers 1: $3^{1}/_{2}$

Health and safety:
Infirmary, RN on staff; doctor in residence at boys' camp; hospital 15 miles away

Concentration:
Susquehannock for Boys: team sports
Susquehannock for Girls: sports, riding, waterfront, arts and crafts

Mission:
"To provide for our campers a healthy, educational, happy summer of group living in the out-of-doors, and to aid in the development of physically and morally strong young men and women who will make good citizens with high ideals."

These brother and sister sports camps are located on separate lakes ten miles apart in the Endless Mountains of northeastern Pennsylvania. They are run by two Shafer brothers (and their wives), whose father founded Susquehannock for Boys in 1905. Combined, the camps take up an area of 2,500 acres, allowing for several wilderness campsites without leaving camp property.

While the boys' camp has a long-standing reputation of being an excellent athletics camp, with a number of intramural teams competing at any given hour of the day, the newer girls' camp concentrates more on lifetime sports instruction than competition.

Susquehannock for Girls is for the girl who may love to play sports but is not necessarily on the varsity at home. Athletics instruction is excellent and meant to develop confidence, not to create all-stars. Everybody participates and has fun. The most popular activity here is horseback riding; second is tennis.

Otherwise, the philosophy of the camps is quite similar. Campers are placed in one of several groups based on overall athletic ability so that they can participate in many sports and games without feeling overmatched or unchallenged by their teammates or the competition. The camps are relaxed, and the top priorities are always the development of self-direction, self-discipline, and sportsmanship.

The centerpiece of Susquehannock for Girls is a handsome fieldstone lodge that contains a large fireplace at one end and a small stage and game room on the other, with banners and camper-made candleholders adorning the walls. Spread out around the campus are cabins, craft shops, a recently built dining hall, gymnastics center, basketball and volleyball courts, playing fields, stables, and riding rings.

The dining hall is served by an excellent new kitchen and decorated with colorful tablecloths and flags from all the campers' home countries. Probably the best feature of dining at either of the camps is that Susquehannock owns and operates a large farm that produces most of the fresh meat and vegetables they serve.

Although athletics and swimming are featured parts of the girls' program, Susquehannock girls can also choose from among a variety of other activities such as campcraft, hiking, overnights, boating, sailing, river canoeing, nature and ecology, the challenge course, arts and crafts, woodworking, drama, singing, dance, gymnastics, and animal care.

Susquehannock for Boys has a variety of fine sports fields and courts, all in first-rate condition. Boys are divided by age into two camps, Junior Camp (7–11) and Hill Camp (12–16), and are further split into nine separate groups according to athletic ability. These groups receive instruction and compete daily in several team sports: soccer, lacrosse, street hockey, baseball, basketball, touch football, and volleyball, with special attention paid to tennis. All campers take instructional swimming and are expected to work toward passing the Red Cross Swimmer's test.

Other activities open to boys include horseback riding, archery, sailing, canoeing, boating, windsurfing, diving, computers, woodworking, tripping, golf, track and field, challenge course, campcraft, fishing, Indian lore, weight training, and Ping-Pong. In addition, there are a variety of special coed activities for which the two camps periodically come together.

Both of the Susquehannock camps, while concentrating on developing athletic skills and sportsmanship in many sports, manage to maintain a close, caring spirit. Everything here is geared toward a family atmosphere in the best sense of the word. Counselors get to know their campers intimately and really care about them. And the kids really seem to care about each other, too. By the end of the session, all the people end up feeling related to each other—not by blood, but by Susquehannock.

Tamarack Tennis Camps

Summer address:
111 Easton Road
Franconia, New Hampshire 03580

Phone:
(603) 823-5656

Winter address:
P.O. Box 518
New Hampton, NH 03256

Phone:
(603) 744-8277

Contact person:
Stephen or Priscilla Fay

Natural features:
Twelve red clay courts located in a mountain range, on 400 acres of forests and rolling hills

Nearest large city or town:
Littleton, NH

Enrollment:
Coed
Boys 50% Girls 50%

Age spread:
10–16

Per summer:
100 (40 per session)

Campers come from the:
Northeast 80% Southeast 10%, Central 2%, Northwest 2%, Southwest 1%, International 5%

Season:
June 23–August 23

Session (by percentage of campers) and cost:
2 weeks, 20%, $1,200
4 weeks, 80%, $2,075

Extra charges:
None

Scholarships:
10% of campers do not pay full tuition

Financial structure:
For profit

Founded:
1962

Owner(s) and years associated with camp:
Jack and Peg Kenney, 33 (founders)

Manager(s) and years associated with camp:
Joanne Kenney, 33

Director(s) and years associated with camp:
Stephen Fay, 6
Priscilla Fay, 9

Directors' backgrounds:
Stephen Fay: B.A., history, University of New Hampshire; teacher and administrator, New Hampton School; 13 years camp experience

Priscilla Fay: B.A., classics, University of New Hampshire; tennis instructor; eight years teaching, administrating, and camp counseling

Counselors: 12
Men 50% Women 50% Min. age 17
Ratio to campers 1: 4

Health and safety:
Infirmary, RN on staff; doctor on call; hospital 15 minutes away

Concentration:
Tennis as a life-long sport for recreation and social fun

Mission:
 "Campers are urged to give to one another and work together in a team environment. Respect and love for others, appreciation of nature, a sense of fair play and an appetite for fun are as important at Tamarack as tennis. The camp's setting, staff, and spirit combine to make it a very special place."

For those youngsters looking for a summer camp that really stresses tennis but that also offers components of a well-rounded general camp, this may be the camp you're looking for. Located at the foot of New Hampshire's Mount Kinsman and close to Franconia Notch and the Old Man in the Mountain, this lovely campus takes in over four hundred acres of rolling fields, streams, and woodlands.

At the center of Tamarack is the camp lodge, which contains bunk rooms, offices, playrooms, living rooms, a kitchen and dining room, a pro shop, and an infirmary. Grouped around the lodge are the camp's twelve clay tennis courts, a trampoline, and a volleyball area. The courts are surrounded by the campers' five rustic cabins, a big red barn used for rainy-day activities, a new professional soccer field, and a pasture for the camp's farm animals.

The founder of Tamarack, Jack Kenney, is one of the founding members of NEPTA (New England Professional Tennis Association) and for thirty-five years has been a well-known and respected tennis instructor. One of the primary strengths of this institution is the fact that Kenney has always managed to staff his camp with talented people who really know how to teach. It's a group that works together and gets along together exceptionally well, and they return to camp each year at the rate of 80 percent.

Campers are separated according to skill into five groups, which receive an average of four hours of tennis instruction every day, the instruction method suitably styled to the particular group. In addition to instruction time, each camper may choose two hours of free tennis time in which to receive more private instruction or participate in various drills. All campers participate in outside matches and Saturday tournaments with surrounding camps, as well as intercamp matches within Tamarack's own tennis ladder. The highlight of the season is a three-day Davis Cup tournament.

Despite the amount of time devoted to tennis and the number of matches campers play, high-intensity competition is not a feature of this camp. And that's what makes Tamarack so successful. Tennis is meant to be fun, and that is how it's taught here. Campers learn first and foremost to be good sports.

Lest you get the impression that all of these youngsters' time is spent on tennis, about a quarter of their schedule is given to more general activities like soccer, ultimate Frisbee, drama, singing, bicycle tours, or swimming at nearby Easton Brook or Echo Lake, in Franconia Notch. Hiking into some of the surrounding high mountains is also a popular activity here.

Friday nights are town nights, when the entire camp travels into nearby Littleton, and on Saturday nights Tamarack puts on dances. There are also special events planned throughout the season, such as Obstacle Course, Haunted House, Three Ball Soccer, etc.

As you might expect in a camp with a demanding physical schedule, Tamarack's menu is well balanced and the food home-cooked, with an emphasis on the natural and nutritious. Parents are asked to refrain from sending sweets in care packages.

This is a small, family-style camp that builds a close-knit community where everyone is genuinely considerate of everyone else. There is little difference here between staff and campers or between younger and older campers. Everybody pulls together to help one another, so that it seems completely natural to find an experienced teenage camper rallying with a ten-year-old. It's the kind of place that can build in a young person the love of a sport for a lifetime.

Camp Tapawingo

Summer address:
Route 93
Sweden, Maine 04040

Phone:
(207) 647-3351
Fax (207) 647-2232

Winter address:
4239 S. 35th Street
P.O. Box 6656
Arlington, VA 22206

Phone:
(703) 820-6404
Fax (703) 820-6405

Natural features:
200 acres (20-acre campus) with lawns leading down to a clear, sandy-bottomed lake

Nearest large city or town:
Located in the southwest corner of Maine, 10 minutes from Bridgton; 30 minutes from North Conway, NH

Enrollment:
Girls

Age spread:
8–16

Per summer:
165

Campers come from the:
Northeast 50% Southeast 25% Central 10% Southwest 3% International 12%

Average number of international campers:
France 2, Mexico 2

Season:
Late June to mid–August

Session (by percentage of campers) and cost:
4 weeks (for first-timers), 10%, $2,850
8 weeks, 90%, $4,950

Extra charges:
Some (riding—$325; uniform)

Scholarships:
2% of campers do not pay full tuition

Financial structure:
For profit

Founded:
1919

Owner/Manager/Director and years associated with camp:
Jane Lichtman, 11

Director's background:
Jane Lichtman: B.S. in psychology, University of Wisconsin; M.A. in administration, Teachers College, Columbia University; served in camping as counselor, department head, food service manager, head counselor; director of Tapawingo since 1984

Counselors: 58
Men 8% Women 92% Min. age 19
Ratio to campers 1: $2^{1}/_{2}$

Health and safety:
Infirmary, doctor and 2 nurses in residence; hospital 10 minutes away

Concentration:
Individualized program; large range of activities, from which each girl chooses her own concentration; historically, Tapawingo has been strong in outdoor tripping (canoe trips, hiking, backpacking), swimming, tennis, drama, arts and crafts, and land sports

Mission:
"We want to help girls improve their self-confidence and skills. We also seek to provide a safe place for girls to learn to be independent of their parents, and to create a second family full of traditions, values, and the support of each person in the community."

This is the kind of camp that ensures that institutionalized camping will remain an important part of the educational growth of many American children. Situated on two hundred acres of forest in the foothills of the White Mountains, the campus is spread over twenty acres of lawns and meadows, playing fields, and bunk houses and other camp buildings, with a mile and a half of shoreline on a crystal-clear lake. The main lodge—a large, handsome building—overlooks the meadow and lake, while twenty-one cabins line the lake shore, each housing eight campers and two counselors.

Tapawingo is a camp devoted to building self-confidence in girls and young women through a program of solid skills instruction. The daily schedule consists of five planned activities plus one free period. While senior campers choose their own activities, junior campers have their programs set for them so that they can experience all that Tapawingo has to offer—and that's a lot. The overall program is built around waterfront activities (instructional and competitive swimming, diving, boating, canoeing, sailing, kayaking, waterskiing, and boardsailing), land sports (softball, tennis, hockey, lacrosse, basketball, volleyball, newcomb, kickball, soccer, archery, track and field, gymnastics, ropes course, and riding), arts and crafts (ceramics, pottery, leather, jewelry, sculpture, painting, drawing, silk-screening, copper enameling, stained glass, macrame, and photography), music and dramatics (chorus, weekly shows, musicals, workshops, improvisational classes, variety shows, and skits; scenery, costumes, makeup, and lighting), and production of a campus newspaper. The camp also offers many sightseeing trips and a special program every evening. Especially noteworthy is Tapawingo's tripping program: more than a hundred trips leave camp each summer, with older campers going out on canoeing and backpacking trips that last up to a week.

Facilities here are outstanding, befitting the top-notch instruction. The tennis program benefits from eight fine tennis courts and tennis practice wall (Tapawingo is a member of the U.S.T.A.). The riding program is served by stables, two riding rings, pastures, and great trails. A sandy, gently sloping beach and excellent dock system are ideal for the camp's ambitious waterfront program.

The camp calls itself a "cheering and singing kind of place," and that's an accurate description. The girls sing grace to start lunch, and after meals are over they sing their favorite camp songs, melodies that have come down through many summers of singing.

"Encouragement, encouragement, and more encouragement," states the camp catalogue, "to assure that the girls develop independence and self-confidence." With a staff-to-camper ratio of $1:2\frac{1}{2}$, this camp makes sure that every girl is well-attended and that she has continuous opportunities to feel proud of her accomplishments and excited about her potentials.

Although the majority of Tapawingo campers are Jewish, the camp is nonsectarian, encouraging campers to live by the "Golden Rule." On Friday evenings campers create a brief ethical service.

People here are the way they should be at camp: involved with one another, friendly, and informal. The camp is consistent. Eighty percent of the campers come back to Tapawingo every year because they know what to expect. Over the course of a summer—and several summers—these girls will grow to mature, talented, and confident young women who have formed the kinds of close friendships that can only be nurtured by a camp like this—friendships that will endure for the rest of their lives.

Teton Valley Ranch Camp

Summer address:
P.O. Box 8
Kelly, Wyoming 83011-0008

Phone:
(307) 733-2958

Winter address:
150 Sylvia Drive
Jackson Hole, WY 83001-9220

Phone:
(307) 733-2958

Natural features:
Large private ranch surrounded by the Bridger-Teton National Forest, the Grand Teton National Park, and the National Elk Refuge; warm-spring-fed pool for swimming

Nearest large city or town:
Jackson; just south of Yellowstone

Enrollment:
Two separate 34-day sessions, one for 125 boys, one for 125 girls

Age spread:
10–16

Per summer:
250

Campers come from the:
Northeast 38% Southeast 8% Central 27% Northwest 4% Southwest 20% International 3%

Average number of international campers:
9—Belgium 3, France 2

Season:
Mid-June to mid-August

Session (by percentage of campers) and cost:
5 weeks, 50% (2 sessions), $2,450

Extra charges:
Some ($150–$200)

Scholarships:
5% of campers do not pay full tuition

Financial structure:
For profit

Founded:
1939

Owner(s) and years associated with camp:
Wendell Wilson family, 53

Managing Director(s) and years associated with camp:
Stuart M. Palmer, 24
Matt Montagne, 28
Susan Palmer, 12

Directors' Backgrounds:
Stuart M. Palmer: B.S., management, University of Arizona

Matt Montagne: B.S., geology, Dartmouth College

Susan Palmer: B.S., wildlife biology, Kansas State University; 2 years staff, Sanborn Western Camps; 2 summers naturalist, Glacier National Park, Montana

Counselors: 24
Men 85% Women 15% (boys' session)
Min. age 19; Ratio to campers 1: 5½
Men 15% Women 85% (girls' session)
Min. age 19; Ratio to Campers 1: 5½

Health and safety:
Infirmary, RN on staff

Concentration:
Horseback riding, wilderness horse pack-tripping, mountain backpacking; outdoor living

Mission:
"Through an active participation in the romance of the Western experience, we hope that every individual will develop and retain a positive character which includes a strong self-image, a respect for others, and an appreciation for the environment."

Teton Valley Ranch Camp is everything a Western ranch summer camp should be and more. As you'd expect, the camp has cattle, a string of good horses, barns, stables, and bunkhouses, but Teton Valley adds several things to the experience: a varied educational program, one of the best swimming pools anywhere—200 yards long, warm-spring-fed, sandy bottomed—and the fact that the campus is bordered by Yellowstone National Park to the north, the Teton mountain range to the west, and the Gros Ventre Mountains to the east. Could there be a better location for a summer camp in America?

More important are Teton Valley's clear goals. "We aim to build a strong self-image in every child," explains director Stuart Palmer. "We won't baby a camper, but we'll bait his or her appetite for the new and different. We strongly encourage each camper to try all aspects of the camp program so they may possibly discover something new that will excite their imagination."

Specifically, these people want every camper to feel comfortable around a horse and capable of riding for long hours at a time or performing in basic horse events that require confidence and control. At the same time, Teton Valley aims for its five-week sessions to develop in all boys and girls the outdoor-living skills that will enable them to be responsible and capable campers.

The camp's free-choice program, as well as its interest in a child's developing self-confidence at his or her own rate, leads to an informal, relaxed atmosphere.

That's not to say these campers don't strive to do their best or take pride in their achievements. In fact, there is a fairly elaborate system of graduated problems to solve and goals to conquer that works on these youngsters' self-motivation in ways that more rigid educational systems can't touch. Once a camper has achieved one level of accomplishment, he or she is naturally encouraged to seek the next higher level.

The staff that implements this program is very well trained. Most are college students, graduate students, teachers, or other professionals who have special talents and interests to offer the campers. Many are Teton Valley alumni.

There are quite a few buildings here, some of which you may not find elsewhere, like the lapidary shop or fly-tying room. Other facilities include three modern bathhouses, a large lodge and dining room, an infirmary, trading post, craft shop, photography darkroom, staff cabins, barns, and storage buildings.

Campers, divided by age, live in log cabins with their counselors. They are also divided into program groups according to ability and experience. Yearlings are the youngest campers at the ranch, having just finished the fifth grade. Rough Riders are first-year campers who have completed the sixth grade or higher. Top Hands are returning campers who have prior experience as Rough Riders. Wranglers have also had at least one year of camping at Teton Valley Ranch; most have been Rough Riders or Top Hands. Trailblazers are the oldest returning campers and participate in the most challenging activities.

Activities include riding, fly-tying and trout fishing, hiking, swimming, riflery, craft work, archery, ham radio, lapidary, photography, roping, music, gymkhana, rodeos, campfire programs, overnight cabin trips, horse pack-trips, backpacking trips, nature discovery activities, trips to Yellowstone, and more. Members of the staff encourage each camper to try everything the ranch has to offer.

Sundays at Teton Valley are special days, beginning with a nondenominational service at the ranch chapel, which overlooks the Gros Ventre River (Catholic campers are driven to Jackson, ten miles away, for Mass). On Sunday afternoon everyone in camp participates in the gymkhana rodeo, which features a host of events, from a water-balloon toss to demanding horse events. Every day ends with a campfire, whether campers are in camp or off on a trip.

At Teton Valley every camper will go out on at least one four- or five-day horse pack-trip into the Teton wilderness or Gros Ventre wilderness area. Complete with professional outfitters, mule strings, and trail cooks, these trips are the Old West at its best. Campers may choose to go backpacking up into the high mountain mead-ows and peaks, too.

However a camper chooses to spend his or her time here, you can be sure that it will be truly valuable. This is one of those places that makes you thankful that such good people have ended up doing such interesting things in such a beautiful place.

Camp Thunderbird for Boys

Camp Thunderbird for Girls

Summer address:
Camp Thunderbird for Boys
Rt. 2, Box 225
Bemidji, Minnesota 56601

Camp Thunderbird for Girls
Rt. 8, Box 532
Bemidji, Minnesota 56601

Phone:
Camp Thunderbird for Boys:
(218) 751–5171
Camp Thunderbird for Girls:
(218) 751–6761

Winter address:
Camp Thunderbird for Boys and Girls
10976 Chamray Court
St. Louis, MO 63141

Phone:
Camp Thunderbird for Boys and Girls
(314) 567–3167

Natural features:
Both camps situated on Lake Plantagenet;
spacious sandy beach, surrounded by a pine
wilderness

Nearest large city or town:
Bemidji

Enrollment:
Boys and girls, in separate camps

Age spread:
8–16

Per summer:
240

Campers come from the:
Northeast 5% Southeast 3% Central 68%
Northwest 8% Southwest 6% International
10%

Average number of international campers:
24—Mexico 12, Canada 4, France 4, Japan 4

Season:
June 20–August 12

Session (by percentage of campers) and cost:
4 weeks, 35%, $2,150
8 weeks, 65%, $3,475

Extra charges:
Some (horseback riding, special trips, rappelling, Canadian fishing)

Financial structure:
For profit

Founded:
Camp Thunderbird for Boys: 1946
Camp Thunderbird for Girls: 1970

Owner(s) and years associated with camp:
Altman family, 48 (founders)

Managing Director(s) and years associated with camp:
Camp Thunderbird for Boys:
Allen L. Sigoloff, 36

Camp Thunderbird for Girls:
Carol A. Sigoloff, 25

Directors' backgrounds:
Allen L. Sigoloff: B.S., recreation and park administration, sociology, University of Illinois

Carol A. Sigoloff: past camper, activity counselor, food-service director, program director; board member for Kiwanis Camp Wyman for Disadvantaged Youth; school board member; classroom volunteer

Counselors:
Camp Thunderbird for Boys: 65
Men 90% Women 10% Min. age 17
Ratio to campers 1: 4

Camp Thunderbird for Girls: 55
Men 10% Women 90% Min. age 17
Ratio to campers 1: 4

Health and safety:
Infirmary, 2 RNs on staff, daily doctor visits, hospital 9 miles away

Concentration:
A multispecialty camp with many activities, from archery and blacksmithing to drama and waterskiing

Mission:
"Thunderbird is a place where children experience challenge without feeling pressured; where they are accepted unconditionally as people of worth. Because Thunderbird is foremost a children's environment, we strive to provide a comfortable arena in which children can freely experience the joy of self-discovery and accomplishment. Learning is fun at Thunderbird. Activities are used to build a child's self-esteem, helping him/her develop skills for later life. In our space-age world of speed and synthetics, exposure to the quiet certainty of woods, water and nature become all the more important for strong young boys and girls to become proud young men and women."

These two camps are separately located high in northern Minnesota's lakes and forests region. Thunderbird for Boys is a four-hundred–acre expanse of towering pines with four and a half miles of sandy beach, while Thunderbird for Girls is situated on two hundred acres of deciduous and pine forest with one mile of sandy beach.

Boys and girls alike live in comfortable cabins, with eight or nine campers and two to four counselors in each. The cabins are clustered in separate "villages," each with a head counselor. While boys have central washrooms, the girls' cabins have private bathrooms. Although the boys and girls each have their own complete facility, a number of special activities bring the two camps together.

The camp calls itself a *multispecialty camp,* meaning that campers choose four activities in which to specialize for their Thunderbird session. At the same time they are encouraged to try as wide a variety of activities as possible in their daily choice of three or four activities.

Campers may select from aerobics, air riflery, archery, arts and crafts, athletics, backpacking, baseball, bicycling, blacksmithing, campcraft, canoeing, drama, fishing, folkcraft, gymnastics, English and western riding, Indian lore, music, nature, newspaper, photo, pottery, riflery, sailboard, sailing, soccer, softball, swimming, tennis, waterskiing, and woodworking.

Twice a week each cabin group plans a "Tribal," an activity that is all theirs, whether that means challenging another cabin to softball or soccer, exploring the creek, using the pontoon boat for fishing or tubing, or just having a fun afternoon on the waterfront. Thunderbird also takes campers on weekly one-day trips, called Adventure Days, to local sight-seeing areas.

Another special activity at Thunderbird is Theme Day. Once a week one of the villages plans an entire day devoted to a theme, such as "Winter Wonderland" or "Greek Olympics." During that day those village campers plan related activities, make decorations, and prepare the camp menu.

Trips at Thunderbird are more challenging than at most camps. Here campers take out a map and plan (with guidance) their own trips, whether by van, horseback, sailboat, bike, canoe, or foot. Although the trips are graduated by difficulty, even the youngest campers go out of camp for up to three nights. Full-session campers are given the opportunity to tour the Mesabi Iron Range, Duluth-North Shore, Thunder Bay, and Winnipeg, Canada. In addition, experienced fifteen- and sixteen-year-old campers may participate in extended trips to the East Coast, Northwest, and Canada.

There's a great energy here that's difficult to identify, but it springs from the culmination of many forces. The institution adheres to old, simple values, and it is carefully and expertly run. The quiet certainty and security of woods, water, and nature, coupled with counselors who really care, make it easy for these youngsters to learn and have fun. The counselors work hard here, and all seem to make a great effort to communicate clearly with the campers and other staff. The result of all of this is a body of campers who are both happy and accountable and who return to Thunderbird year after year at the rate of nearly 85 percent. That's as good a barometer of a camp's true value as you'll find.

Camp Timanous

Summer address:
RFD, Plains Road
Raymond, Maine 04071

Phone:
(207) 655-4569

Winter address:
St. Mark's School
Southboro, MA 01772

Phone:
(508) 485-8020
Fax (508) 460-6164

Natural features:
Situated on Panther Pond, heavily timbered with pine, bordered by a 1,000-foot mountain

Nearest large city or town:
Portland

Enrollment:
Boys

Age spread:
7–15

Per summer:
120

Campers come from the:
Northeast 59% Southeast 4% Central 26% Southwest 1% International 10%

Average number of international campers:
12—France 5, Mexico 4, Venezuela 4

Season:
June 25–August 13

Session (by percentage of campers) and cost:
4 weeks, 20%, $2,600
7 weeks, 80%, $3,650

Extra charges:
Some (uniforms—$200; medical insurance—$80)

Financial structure:
For profit

Founded:
1916

Owner(s) and years associated with camp:
David W. Suitor, 34

Managing Director(s) and years associated with camp:
David W. Suitor, 34

Director's background:
David W. Suitor: B.A., University of Vermont; faculty, St. Mark's School, Massachusetts

Counselors: 35
Men 92% Women 8% Min. age 16
Ratio to campers 1: 3$^1/_3$

Health and safety:
Infirmary, 2 RNs on staff; hospital nearby

Concentration:
Sailing, wood shop, tennis, campcraft, riflery, swimming

Mission:

"The training of the body, mind, and spirit. The MIND is made inquisitive and challenged by a program which includes more than a dozen regularly scheduled activities, a competent and friendly staff, and suitable recognition for incentive. The BODY is developed and strengthened by exercise, rest, good food and outdoor living. The SPIRIT is nourished by a non-sectarian chapel service Sunday morning and the weekly Council Fire on Sunday evening, coupled with a fine tradition of courteous, loyal and respectful relationship between boys and staff."

Timanous is located on 180 acres of land on the shores of Panther Pond, in the Sebago Lake area of southern Maine. Nearly a mile of shore frontage includes a sheltered cove, beaches, and deep water for safe diving. Directly behind the heavily pined living area, a 1,000-foot mountain rises, offering climbers a broad vista of the entire Sebago area.

It's a campus designed to feel spacious, with the ball field, cabins, and recreation lodge down by the lakeside, and other activity areas spread out behind in partially wooded areas. Although the atmosphere is natural and woodsy, campers' T-shirt uniforms are always clean and their cabins immaculately neat. Walking around, I'm reminded of a collection of small beehives, there's so much concentrated activity going on.

"Timanous is not a luxury camp," states the camp's brochure. "There is neither electricity nor hot water in cabins. . . . Our emphasis is on the benefits to the boys of a simple, healthful life among friendly, interested, and capable people."

Neither is this a camp that eschews competition. Achievement is important here. The camp sees its role as preparing boys to enter a world where competition is a reality, and they aim to prepare the campers to approach challenges with "poise and confidence." At the same time, the camp stresses sportsmanship and courtesy and is always generous in its recognition of all of its campers, commending boys at Sunday Council Fires even for minor achievements.

The Timanous program is an even mixture of assigned and free-choice activities in a daily schedule that includes two assigned periods and two periods of elective activities. Swimming instruction is mandatory and offered in graded courses, from basic instruction to nonswimmers through lifesaving and water-aide training for the most advanced groups.

Many of the activities have a competitive component built in. For example, the Timanous archery team competes in matches with other camps. There are three baseball teams, made up of ten-and-under, twelve-and-under, and fourteen-and-under age groups, which play intercamp games; and there's an intercamp softball league open to all ages. The Timanous riflemen compete in matches with other camps, as do teams in tennis, soccer, and swimming.

The Timanous fleet consists of six MIT fiberglass racing dinghies and a Winabout for the more advanced sailors, as well as a number of Windsurfers. Twenty canoes range from 12-footers to 24-foot war canoes, which carry ten people. The camp also owns rowboats for fishing and two paddleboats for fun. Every Timanous boy receives sailing instruction, culminating in his participation in weekly sailing races on Sebago Lake and in regattas on Panther Pond.

The camp has a fine campcraft program, with trips ranging from one to five nights traveling to Sebago Lake, the White Mountain National Forest, and the Rangeley Lakes region. All trips are preceded by in-camp instruction conducted by the trip counselors. Other activities include crafts and woodshop, dramatics and music, nature and ecology, and waterskiing.

Timanous properly places a great deal of emphasis on the quality of its counselor staff, 75 percent of whom are former Timanous campers and many of whom are teachers. Cabins consist of a head counselor, senior counselor, and junior counselor, along with eleven campers.

What's most impressive to me about this camp, especially considering its sheer amount of physical activity, is that Timanous's educational values far outweigh athletic and skills goals. An ongoing attempt is made to synthesize body, mind, and spirit while instilling sharing, cooperation, and honesty in the boys. People get lots of praise, both in public and in private, and that praise goes a long way toward encouraging future effort. As in many other fine camps, sometimes the numbers tell the story best. At Timanous about 75 percent of the campers and 90 percent of the staff return year after year, and you can't do much better than that.

Camp Virginia, Inc.

CAMP VIRGINIA

Summer address:
Goshen, Virginia 24439

Phone:
(703) 997-5977

Winter address:
8122 Greystone Circle
Richmond, VA 23229

Phone:
(804) 282-2339

Natural features:
55 acres of flat fields in the Alleghenies,
bounded by the Maury River and the Goshen Wildlife Area

Nearest large city or town:
Between Staunton and Lexington

Enrollment:
Boys

Age spread:
8–15

Per summer:
188

Campers come from the:
Northeast 5% Southeast 90%, International
5%

Average number of international campers:
Russia 5, France 3, Spain 2

Season:
June 23–August 4

Session (by percentage of campers) and cost:
3 weeks, 70%, $1,500
6 weeks, 30%, $2,400

Scholarships:
6% of campers do not pay full tuition

Extra charges:
Some (insurance, uniform, laundry—$100–$150)

Financial structure:
For profit

Founded:
1928

Owner(s) and years associated with camp:
Malcolm U. Pitt, 66
Betty Pitt, 46

Director(s) and years associated with camp:
Malcolm U. Pitt, 66

Director's background:
Malcolm U. Pitt: B.A., University of Richmond; M.Ed., Harvard, University of Virginia; school administration; president, the Collegiate Schools, Richmond

Counselors: 25
Men 100% Min. age 19
Ratio to campers 1: 4

Health and safety:
Infirmary, doctor and RN on staff; hospital nearby

Concentration:
Skills and attitudes; athletics, swimming, riding, camping

Mission:
"Reaching each camper and helping him grow as a well-rounded person. The spiritual opportunities are there because of our surroundings and role models. We feed the campers well and
provide for rest as well as activity, helping them improve physically. In teaching unselfishness and
how to get along with others, social skills are developed. Finally, acquiring greater appreciation
for God, family, friends and our nation."

Although Camp Virginia is surrounded by the rugged Allegheny Mountains,
the campus itself sits on fifty-four acres of flat and fertile countryside that is
wonderfully secluded. Bordered by the cool, clean Maury River, on the camp side
of the river there are no neighbors for three miles; beyond the river is the 2,600-
acre Goshen Wildlife Area. These are vast, uninhabited lands, a perfect environment for a boys' camp like Virginia.

The camp makes intelligent use of its land. Situated in shaded areas are riflery,
archery, and campcraft areas, and the riding stables. In the open, flat areas are fields
for soccer and lacrosse, three baseball diamonds, and six hard-surface tennis courts.

The buildings, in keeping with the camp's philosophy, are not flashy, but perfectly utilitarian and in excellent shape. (As a matter of fact, 1985 brought the worst
flood in the area's history and forced the replacing of seventeen buildings; the
camp's alumni association gave $75,000 to the task.)

Campers are assigned to cabins and lodges at a ratio of one counselor to every
four campers. There are separate buildings for the crafts shop, indoor basketball,
and general recreation, as well as Memorial Hall, which hosts camp gatherings,
church services, and movies. There are also a shower building and new bathroom
facilities.

Camp Virginia offers an uninterrupted six-week session or a split session for the
first or last three weeks. Regardless of short or long session, all campers receive
sound instruction in a host of traditional camp activities. While every camper is
assigned to all of the activities on a regular schedule, he is also given plenty of free
time to concentrate on some of his favorites.

In addition to athletics, each camper learns water safety and horseback riding (an overnight horseback hike highlights this activity). Many campers go canoeing and fishing during the after-dinner optional time. Movies and Ping-Pong are also welcome changes in pace.

The staff here is older and noticeably more mature than at most camps. It is an advantage that is telling in many ways, but particularly in the overseeing of individual campers. Counselors assess each boy's skills, attitude, and spirit each week. In addition, the lodge counselor is responsible for writing weekly evaluations of each of his five boys' overall progress.

As you'd expect, the dining hall is sound, efficient, and well equipped. Food is good, nutritious, plentiful, and varied, prepared by college-trained cooks.

Supported by a solid, unwavering structure, Virginia is a traditional camp that provides the best features of a small camp atmosphere and one that also reflects the best of Southern life. It's a warm, easy, and personable place, one in which people express a genuine affection for one another. Integrity, unselfishness, and gratitude are stressed in all phases of life, especially in the activities, and these values are enhanced by daily devotions and prayers.

There are no surprises here. The camp philosophy, which has been a force in the lives of three generations of campers, has not wavered from its founding beliefs, and today's managers do not anticipate any changes in the foreseeable future. In its attempt to provide a strong and enduring camp atmosphere, Camp Virginia succeeds admirably. This is a home away from home where boys can feel comfortable and confident, and a place where every boy can make many lasting friendships.

Camp Waldemar

waldemar camp for girls

Address:
Rt. 1, Box 120
Hunt, Texas 78024

Phone:
(210) 238-4821

Natural features:
Located in Texas Hill Country, on the Guadalupe River; 550 acres at 2,000 feet elevation

Nearest large city or town:
Kerrville, San Antonio

Enrollment:
Girls

Age spread:
7–16

Per summer:
824

Campers come from the:
Northeast 2% Southeast 10% Central 1%
Northwest 2% Southwest 85%

Season:
June 2–August 25

Session (by percentage of campers) and cost:
7 days, 24%, $700
5 weeks, 76%, $2,300

Extra charges:
Some (extras—$100, charge account)

Financial structure:
For profit

Founded:
1926

Owner(s) and years associated with camp:
Marsha Elmore, 44

Managing Director(s) and years associated with camp:
Marsha Elmore, 44

Director's background:
Marsha Elmore: graduate, Southern Methodist University; owner/director of Waldemar since 1979

Counselors: 100
Women 100% Min. age 18
Ratio to campers 1: 3

Health and safety:
Infirmary, 3 RNs on staff

Concentration:
"The total development of each camper in spiritual, philosophical and physical growth." A variety of 35 activities, from ceramics to fencing, swimming, and horseback riding.

Mission:
"We instill the highest ideals and values, a love and respect for God's world, starting with each other. To make each camper feel like she is cared for and successful in what she attempts to do her best in. And to make campers proficient in the activities they choose to take."

Camp Waldemar is a gorgeous facility that looks more like a vacation resort than a girls' camp. Located on the banks of the Guadalupe River, in the heart of Texas Hill Country, the two-thousand-acre campus features a plethora of trees and plants, from cactus to five-hundred-year-old cypress trees, on grounds that are so well kept they seem practically manicured. The thirty or more stone buildings, the exquisite amphitheater, and the lodge on the cypress-lined riverbank all contribute to give the camp a solid, venerable feeling, not unlike the philosophy that has driven this camp since its inception.

Waldemar places heavy emphasis on the teaching of skills, with a staff committed to guiding its campers to be successful, respectable, and upright citizens. "If we can affect the values of these girls," says Marsha Elmore, "they will make the world a better place. These girls have a tremendous potential to be leaders."

The girls of Waldemar are grouped by age and live seven to a cabin (known as "kampongs") along with a counselor who serves as "mother" to the group. Each girl is awarded daily points for keeping clothes and belongings in order, sweeping, mopping, and sharing other housekeeping duties.

Campers are allowed to choose from thirty-five or more activities that are offered daily in the areas of land sports, water sports, arts and crafts, chorus, dance, and drama. Five activities and two alternates are chosen, and girls attend these classes daily. Included are: archery, badminton, tennis, fencing, gymnastics, volleyball, basketball, riding, riflery, softball, golf (driving range and putting green), and soccer, with classes for beginning, intermediate, and advanced levels. The camp's staff of water-safety instructors supervises lessons in swimming, diving, lifesaving, and canoeing. Horseback riding is taught both western and English style, on the camp's quarter horses, Arabians, and Appaloosas. At the end of camp, the riding department stages a grand horse show in which riders compete individually.

The arts program offers instruction in drawing, painting, weaving and stitchery, ceramics, jewelry making, dance, drama, and chorus. Drama is divided into junior and senior sections, with each group responsible for one full-scale production during the session. Besides receiving acting lessons, campers are taught how to use lighting, construct sets, and design costumes.

The 310 girls who attend Waldemar each term are divided into three tribes: the Aztecs, the Tejas, and the Comanches. On weekly tribal hill nights, the girls climb to their tribe's secret gathering place, where they conduct a spiritual campfire program to recognize campers' individual achievements. On Field Day, three huge war canoes carry eleven girls each down the Gaudalupe in a celebrated camp race.

On Sunday mornings, interdenominational church services are held, and on Sunday nights each tribe conducts a vesper service in the chapel under the stars.

Waldemar is a first-class, financially sound institution that always manages to provide an extra touch. Six of its eight tennis courts are lighted for evening play. Meals are prepared by a chef with outstanding credentials and consist of top-notch, often gourmet fare: shrimp, fresh fruit and vegetables, crepes and soufflés, home-made breads and desserts.

This is a place that is deeply, and without apology, steeped in tradition. The old stone buildings, the venerable grounds, the director, and the staff all work together to instill in the girls a reverence for the past and a belief in the old values: good manners, cleanliness, and respect for others, all of this without losing sight of the manifold opportunities of the twentieth and twenty-first centuries.

Camp Wawenock

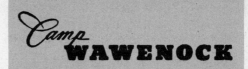

Address:
33 Camp Wawenock Road
Raymond, Maine 04071-6824

Phone:
(207) 655-4657

Natural features:
Located on 75 acres of open fields, woodlands, and sandy beach on Sebago Lake, Maine's second-largest lake

Nearest large city or town:
Portland, Windham

Enrollment:
Girls

Age spread:
8–16

Per summer:
110

Campers come from the:
Northeast 65% Southeast 5% Central 19% Northwest 1% Southwest 1% International 9%

Average number of international campers:
10—Dominican Republic 5, Canada 3, Russia 2

Season:
June 29–August 16

Session (by percentage of campers) and cost:
7 weeks, 100%, $3,350

Extra charges:
Some (riding)

Scholarships:
7% of campers do not pay full tuition

Financial structure:
For profit

Founded:
1910

Owners/Managers and years associated with camp:
June W. Gray, 37
Patricia A. Smith, 27

Director(s) and years associated with camp:
June W. Gray, 37
Patricia A. Smith, 27

Directors' backgrounds:
June W. Gray: B.S., physical education; graduate work in education; teacher in private and public schools and at the college level; certified camp director

Patricia A. Smith: B.S., physical education; M.Ed., education; certified camp director

Counselors: 40
Men 5% Women 95% Min. age 19
Ratio to campers 1: 3

Health and safety:
Infirmary, resident nurse; physician on call; hospital less than 30 minutes away

Concentration:
General camp program, with emphasis on riding and leadership training for older campers and CITs

Mission:

"Wawenock believes in health and happiness, athletic skills, social adjustment, individual resourcefulness, well-rounded development of abilities and an appreciation of the worthwhile things in life. . . . We want to help each person develop her best self through group interaction. . . . We take seriously our intent to preserve and be good stewards of our camp setting and physical plant for future generations."

There is something special about this lakes region of Maine and summer camps. So many old and valuable camps operate on these shores that one might suspect—perhaps rightly so—that they feed off one another.

Wawenock is a seven-week girls' camp that preserves in every way the best of camping tradition. Founded by an educator in 1910, the camp has remained under the continuous direction of educators since that time. It's hard to imagine any institution could be more carefully managed.

The setting is ideal: majestic lake, sandy beach, cabins dotting the shore, the White Mountains reaching up in the distance. The campus is thoughtfully designed to make best use of its resources. Senior girls live in cabins along the waterfront. Middlers and sub-seniors stay in hillside cabins, while Junior girls live in a lodge with their own living room and fireplace.

The activities program is educational in every way, structured on sound skills progression. Campers receive first-rate instruction each day in four free-choice activities selected from a menu that includes riding, tennis, swimming, canoeing, sailing, music, drama, dancing, crafts, art, ceramics, archery, and riflery. Camping, outdoor living skills and canoe trips are also offered.

Wawenock's riding program is particularly strong, enhanced by top-notch stables, riding rings, and groomed trails that are indicative of the care given to the entire institution. The camp is host to several nearby girls' camps at the annual Lake Sebago Horse Show and holds its own show for those who ride at camp.

The tennis program, also noteworthy, is served by four all-weather courts, a practice court, and a ball machine. Instruction in swimming, lifeguard training, canoeing, and sailing is based on the Red Cross program. Sailors take part in regattas with nearby boys' and girls' camps.

The theater, library, recreation hall, and craft shop are housed in Owaissa, a venerable lakefront building with a massive stone fireplace. The dining hall, called Wawenock, is a metaphor for the camp: friendly, neat, traditional, with all the charm of well-tended old age. Campers and counselors sit together, eight to a table, surrounded by plaques and team banners from years gone by. A comfortable happiness predominates, considerate but not restrained. Girls are singing, laughing, talking.

Outside, the same feeling predominates. Down at the lakeshore, girls are swimming and shouting and laughing, while a lawn mower whirs busily nearby. At Wawenock, you are constantly surrounded by courteous people celebrating the tradition of considerate, careful outdoor education.

What makes this camp work so well is the unwavering dedication of everyone to the important things: character, simplicity, and values. The directors, who live here year-round, know all of the campers and counselors personally. Campers come back year after year and look forward to taking leadership roles. There is hardly any staff turnover. Counselors, almost without exception, are former Wawenock campers, and they are unabashed in their enthusiasm for what this place is all about. In fact, the entire staff exhibits such a powerful commitment to the spirit and principles of this camp that it's impossible to envision Wawenock ever ceasing to inhabit this lakeside in precisely the way it has for the last eight decades.

Windridge Tennis Camps

Summer address:
Box 27
Craftsbury Common, Vermont 05827

Phone:
(802) 586-9646

Winter address:
Box 463
Richmond, VT 05477

Phone:
(802) 434-2505

Natural features:
A mix of open fields, hardwood forest, and winding lakefront; tennis courts and common buildings are spread on an overlooking ridge

Nearest large city or town:
Hardwick; northwest of St. Johnsbury

Enrollment:
Coed
Boys 50% Girls 50%

Age spread:
10–15

Per summer:
325

Campers come from the:
Northeast 72% Southeast 2% Central 2% Northwest 1% Southwest 2% International 21%

Average number of international campers:
51—Canada 32, France 5, Spain 4, England 3

Season:
June 11–August 23

Session (by percentage of campers) and cost:
June: 19 days, $1,450
July: 31 days, $2,800
August: 18 days, $1,600

Extra charges:
Taxi fare from airport; laundry

Scholarships:
5% of campers do not pay full tuition

Financial structure:
For profit

Founded:
1968

Owner(s) and years associated with camp:
Alden Bryan, 17
Ted Hoehn, 17
Charles Blauvelt, 17
Eric Walka, 17

Managing Director(s) and years associated with camp:
Charles Witherell, 20

Other Director(s) and years associated with camp:
Paul Baker Dayton, 7
Rosalind Kermode, 4

Directors' backgrounds:
Charles Witherell: B.S., Cornell University; former recreation director; school board director; Cub Scout pack leader

Paul Baker Dayton: B.A., Colorado College; former tennis pro; tennis and squash coach, Bowdoin College; USPTA teaching professional

Rosalind Kermode: B.S., Rice University; master's in sports administration, University of Massachusetts; head tennis coach, Bowdoin College

Counselors: 30
Men 50% Women 50% Min. age 18
Ratio to campers 1: 3.6

Health and safety:
Infirmary; nurse on call; medical center 20 minutes away

Concentration:
Tennis; also an active waterfront program: canoeing, sailing, swimming; theater, soccer, archery

Mission:
"To provide campers with instruction, activities, care and good fun so they are assured a happy and rewarding experience. We believe that children who are encouraged to do well in areas they enjoy will show a positive personality growth. Within this idealized community, children discover the meaning of trust and respect for others, and they are able to realize a confidence in themselves as well as a good feeling toward those around them."

By its very name, you'd guess that Windridge is another one of a multitude of specialty camps that were born in the past three decades. But don't be fooled. This is a fine New England camp with a wide range of offerings and a happy, active group of youngsters to testify to its success. Yes, it does concentrate on tennis, but no more than some of the other camps in this book concentrate on, say, swimming or tripping.

There are two Windridge camps (the other, equally worthy, is in Teela-Wooket, combining its tennis with ambitious riding and soccer programs), but the one I chose to feature is located in Craftsbury Common, high in the mountains of Vermont's Northeast Kingdom and spread out over fifty-two acres around a beautiful lake.

Situated off a rural road in the green and rolling foothills, the campus is a delightful mixture of rustic buildings and first-rate facilities that include fourteen tennis courts, an indoor tennis training center, a large backboard, three ball machines, and a mile-long waterfront along a protected cove, which features a diving area and a wonderful rooftop water slide. Campers live in twenty-six lakefront cabins, each supervised by a counselor.

One reason for Windridge's escaping the tag of "specialty camp" is its sensible hiring of counselors. These people are not tennis instructors who happen to live with their campers; they are counselors who have learned how to play tennis, many of them right here at Windridge. Teaching young people how to get along with others and appreciate themselves is what this camp is about.

Most of the time, boys and girls of all ages participate in activities together. The older students learn how to help the younger, and the younger learn to model the behavior of the older, who in turn model the behavior of the counselors. It's a system that works terrifically and is a delightful thing to witness.

All campers have tennis instruction a minimum of two and a half hours per day. It's excellent instruction, offering a solid foundation for young players while it challenges advanced players to improve both their strokes and strategy. The teaching is patient and personal, making each new skill easy to learn and easy to retain, thus helping to develop confidence in these campers right from the start.

In addition to tennis, Windridge boys and girls may choose from many other activities, such as sailing, swimming, snorkeling, canoeing, dramatic productions, dance and other performing arts, candle-making, drawing, clay sculpture, tie-dying, macrame, and photography, as well as opportunities for overnight canoe trips, hiking into the Green Mountains, and fishing. Evenings are reserved for all-camp activities such as campfire gatherings, stage productions, or weekly dances.

Meals at Windridge are terrific. There are bakers here who bake the bread and make desserts, and professional cooks who prepare three fresh and nutritious meals a day, served family-style in a very pleasant, homey dining room.

Since its first summer in 1968, boys and girls have come from all fifty states and thirty foreign countries. There is a friendly family feeling to this camp, as well as a very strong instructional program for boys and girls who love the game of tennis. They learn to improve their own game by learning concentration and receiving lots of playing time, and they learn a lot about themselves and their relationship to others in the bargain.

Camp Winnebago

Summer address:
Kents Hill, Maine 04349

Phone:
(207) 685-4918

Winter address:
1606 Washington Plaza
Reston, VA 22090

Phone:
(703) 471-1705

Natural features:
Stately pines, gently sloping land to a clear,
three-mile-long lake

Nearest large city or town:
Augusta, Winthrop

Enrollment:
Boys

Age spread:
8–15

Per summer:
160 (140 per session)

Campers come from the:
Northeast 60% Southeast 26% Central 2%
Northwest 2% Southwest 2% International
8%

**Average number of international
campers:**
13—France 4, Colombia 2, England 2,
Spain 2

Season:
June 25–August 18

**Session (by percentage of campers)
and cost:**
4 weeks, 25%, $3,100
8 weeks, 75%, $5,150

Extra charges:
Some (laundry, some trips)

Scholarships:
10% of campers do not pay full tuition

Financial structure:
For profit

Founded:
1919

**Owner/Director and years associated
with camp:**
Phil Lilienthal, 50

Director's background:
Phil Lilienthal: B.A., Amherst College;
U.B., University of Virginia; as Peace Corps
volunteer (1965–67), established the first
permanent residential children's camp in
Ethiopia

Counselors: 50
Men 80% Women 20% Min. age 19
Ratio to campers 1: 3

Health and safety:
Infirmary, doctor and nurse in residence;
hospital 15 minutes away

Concentration:
Traditional camp program stressing human
relationships

Mission:

"We accept each boy for what he has to offer and seek to make each feel comfortable at his own level of skills and interests. . . . A boy's full use of his capacity matters more to us than winning. In every team or individual sport and in every activity we stress effort, improvement and, of course, achievement. We do this through staff encouragement, expert instruction and rewards for accomplishment."

The best of both worlds is what you find here: the wide range of activities of a big camp set in a small-camp atmosphere. Camp Winnebago resides in an abundance of tall pines on the shores of Echo Lake in central Maine. The camp's old Victorian buildings overlook top-notch playing fields, with a fine waterfront nearby.

Boys live in cabins and use the larger halls for dining, recreation, and assemblies. Among the buildings are a fitness center, with weights and machines, a 500-volume library, a Ping-Pong building that is always open, an arts and crafts building, and more. The waterfront contains a dock with six swim lanes, water slide, high dive, eight sailboats, 22 canoes, and a number of kayaks and Windsurfers.

The daily schedule is carefully arranged to allow for three types of activities: athletic, waterfront, and free-selection activities (described as "lifelong skills," such as sailing, campcraft, or photography). A boy will progress through the skill levels of two free-selection activities for a twelve-day period, and then he is free to choose two more. Athletics and swimming continue for every camper throughout the season.

Athletic activities are particularly numerous, among them tennis, windsurfing, volleyball, campcraft, archery, baseball, softball, riflery, soccer, basketball, floor hockey, tetherball, Ping-Pong, ropes course, swimming, diving, canoeing, kayaking, and waterskiing. In addition, Winnebago runs an extensive trips program designed to broaden a camper's perspective of camp, camping, and his peers. Each age group goes on two trips, from three to ten days in duration.

Sports are all taught with a high level of proficiency, and there are lots of opportunities for competition. Boys are divided by age groups into two dozen teams that compete in friendly games against one another daily, as well as against other camps and in intercamp tournaments. Winning is not what is most important to these people, however, but sportsmanship.

"By involvement in competitive activities," explains director Phil Lilienthal, "we encourage campers to support and cooperate with each other. But we are quick to stop any player from denigrating another or putting him down in any way."

Along with athletics, Winnebago also offers a full line of noncompetitive endeavors such as arts and crafts (tie-dye, stained glass, pottery, woodworking, drawing, and painting), newspaper, and video productions. Explains Lilienthal, "We hope that by exposure to many noncompetitive activities, they will see the value of the creative, expressive, or disciplined areas involved."

Everybody here is active and happy. Boys (who call their counselors, affectionately, "Uncle" and "Aunt") value this camp because it is what is says it is: a place where people are rewarded for trying their best, and where they are secure because they can count on others for help if they need it. The slogan here is "Winnebago is not for the boy who can, but the boy who will."

Winona Camps for Boys

Summer address:
RR1, Box 868
Bridgton, Maine 04009-9774

Phone:
(207) 647-3721
Fax (207) 647-2750

Winter address:
RFD 1, Box 868
Bridgton, ME 04009

Phone:
same

Natural features:
Located on Moose Pond, with a mile of waterfront and 400 acres of woods and streams

Nearest large city or town:
Northwest of Sebago Lake

Enrollment:
Boys

Age spread:
8–16

Per summer:
275

Campers come from the:
Northeast 47% Southeast 6% Central 4% Northwest 1% Southwest 2% International 40%

Average number of international campers:
67—France 12, Venezuela 14, Spain 14, France 12, Mexico 11, Germany 8, Dominican Republic 4, Italy 4

Season:
Late June to mid-August

Session (by percentage of campers) and cost:
3¹/₂ weeks, 38%, $2,375
7 weeks, 62%, $3,975

Extra charges:
None

Scholarships:
11% of campers do not pay full tuition

Financial structure:
For profit

Founded:
1908—Winona for Boys and Wyonegonic for Girls are the oldest brother/sister camps in the United States

Owner(s) and years associated with camp:
Alan Ordway, 36
Michelle S. Ordway, 26

Director(s) and years associated with camp:
Alan Ordway, 36
Michelle S. Ordway, 26

Directors' backgrounds:
Alan Ordway: B.A., Yale University; 26 years camp director

Michelle S. Ordway: B.A., Vassar College; 26 years camp director

Counselors: 59
Men 95% Women 5% Min. age 17
Ratio to campers 1: 3

Health and safety:
Infirmary, RNs on staff; hospital 10 minutes
away

Concentration:
The three strongest activity programs are
riding, sailing, and wilderness trips (both canoe and mountain); twelve to fifteen activities offered per day

Mission:
 "The freedom to choose, to explore new activities and to gain expertise in one or more
activities on a daily basis is one of the things that makes our camp unique. . . . Everyone
participates. This is not a place for spectators."

Winona is located on approximately four hundred acres of wooded land
along the eastern shore of Moose Pond. The camp's waterfront stretches
for about one mile, offering two separate swimming areas, a sailing center, and
docks for kayaking and canoeing. The campsites also run along the shore, divided
by age into four separate units, each unit with its own director, head counselor, and
facilities.

The hub of each unit is a large, open-air building known as the *wiggy,* a very
busy place, to say the least. Assemblies, Ping-Pong tables, rainy-day games, pianos,
mail, activity charts, merit achievement lists, books, laundry, and visitors are all
found at the wiggy. Close by are platform tents, each of which houses five campers
and a counselor. Two toilet facilities and a shower building are also found in each
unit. Buildings common to the entire camp include a theater, dining hall/office,
health center, arts and crafts facility, and a multipurpose area. Befitting Winona's
program, facilities are purposely rustic but always neat and tidy.

This camp is exemplary in many ways. It has a large international representation
and a generous scholarship program, both of which ensure a strong diversity in the
boys who come here. With a turnover rate of only 10 to 15 percent, Winona's staff
is among the most solid in my research, no accident given the heavy emphasis
placed on staff training and certification. The people who work here really care for
their campers. They know them as people, as family, and as friends.

Young and older campers alike work toward three merit awards by achieving a
basic level of competence in swimming, canoeing, and campcraft. Campers design
the remainder of their individual programs with counselor guidance. For example,

a boy may decide that he wants to go on a three- to five-day mountain trip, so a counselor works with other staff members to help schedule it in. In the same way, a senior camper may sign up for a ten-day canoe trip up the hundred-mile Allagash Wilderness Waterway in northern Maine, or any number of other trips.

The program is both educational and recreational, more or less centered around three strong programs: riding, sailing, and wilderness trips. Activities include swimming, canoeing, rowing, sailing, and windsurfing; baseball, soccer, tennis, archery, and riflery; campcraft, ecology, canoe and mountain trips, and technical rock climbing; arts and crafts, industrial arts, photography, and horseback riding. There is some competition, particularly in the athletic activities, but the emphasis is always on participating, never winning. One thing that boys learn here is how to win—and lose—with grace.

There are also many special events, such as coed play days with sister camp Wyonegonic, movie nights, make-your-own-banana-splits, etc. Special tutoring (at an extra charge) may be obtained in most subjects in a way that does not interfere with a camper's other activities.

The dining hall seats all campers and staff at one sitting, and meals are served family-style. Such times are always busy, yet even with all the activity, these boys are naturally polite and considerate to one another. It's simply the way things are done here.

Winona has been around for a long time because it has worlds of integrity, and it will last a long time to come because of the loyalty of its alumni. This is a purposeful and deeply committed institution, and as fine an example of a youth camp as you're likely to find—so well managed, in fact, that its structure is practically invisible. What seems like lots of spontaneity is actually the result of very careful planning. When I asked director Alan B. Ordway for a statement of the camp's goals and values, he responded this way:

Winona is a group of people exploring the very restlessness of human nature. Campers are not pressed by time in any abstract sense. Instead, they can rediscover natural rhythms . . . paddling a canoe, walking a trail, singing a song, watching the stars.

We safeguard a vital legacy of spontaneity and discovery. Ideals are fashioned free from the narrowness of bureaucracy. We provide direction—provoking, not imposing, form on a young person's awakening sense of self.

Throughout the seven weeks at Winona a boy learns new skills, makes lasting friendships, and grows physically stronger. Accomplishments, even if small or unnoticed at the time, add up daily. But what motivates him, especially after his camping session is over, is a stronger sense of accountability for his actions.

The challenge facing Winona remains to preserve a sense of earned accomplishment and perseverance over instant gratification; to encourage let-me-experiment attitudes over show-me boredom; and to replace fragmentation that characterizes many activities of young people with a renewed sense of patience and concentration.

Wohelo–Luther Gulick Camps

Address:
P.O. Box 39
South Casco, Maine 04077

Phone:
(207) 655-4739
Fax (207) 655-2292

Natural features:
A mile of shoreline on Sebago Lake, with two sandy beaches, several grassy fields and a beautiful view across the lake to the White Mountains

Nearest large city or town:
Raymond

Enrollment:
Girls

Age spread:
6–12 Little Wohelo
12–16 Sebago Wohelo

Per summer:
180

Campers come from the:
Northeast 62% Southeast 15% Central 6% Northwest 1% Southwest 1% International 15%

Average number of international campers:
20—Venezuela 8, France 4, Japan 3, Canada 2

Season:
June 24–August 12

Session (by percentage of campers) and cost:
3$^{1}/_{2}$ weeks, 15%, $2,450
7 weeks, 85%, $3,800

Extra charges:
Some (uniforms)

Financial structure:
For profit

Founded:
1907

Owner(s) and years associated with camp:
Davis Van Winkle, 25
Louise Gulick Van Winkle, 49

Managing Director(s) and years associated with camp:
Davis Van Winkle, 25
Louise Gulick Van Winkle, 49

Other Director(s) and years associated with camp:
Evelyn Hewson King, 30

Directors' backgrounds:
Davis Van Winkle: B.A., Middlebury College; teacher and coach, Kents Hill School, Waynflete School and Bates College, all in Maine; former president, Youth Camping Association

Louise Gulick Van Winkle: B.A., Middlebury College; grew up as camper/counselor at Wohelo; former board and executive committee member, American Camping Association; board member, Maine Youth Camping Association

Evelyn Hewson King: B.A., Bowdoin College; former camper/counselor at Wohelo; 2 years as director of Little Wohelo

Counselors: 70
Men 7% Women 93% Min. age 16
Ratio to campers 1: 3½

Health and safety:
Infirmary, RN on staff; hospital ½ hour away

Concentration:
Swimming, boating, and other activities geared toward lifetime skills; older girls may specialize in any one area

Mission:
"Our aim is to create an environment of relaxed friendliness close to nature. We want a simple environment, away from the conveniences and complications of the modern world, where personal growth is a central focus and the campers are getting education through experience. We feel the summer would be wonderful if every camper went home with one of the following three things: she made a friend; she learned a new skill which might be useful throughout her life; she had fun."

Sebago Lake is one of New England's most beautiful bodies of water, and Wohelo occupies a mile of its shore, tucked into a large cove with two sandy beaches and a beautiful view across the lake toward the White Mountains. The campus consists of three hundred acres of forest and grassy fields, with three islands and a camping ground on the Crooked River. It's a place with a rich heritage in the world of American camping. This is where the Camp Fire Girls was founded.

Wohelo is actually two separate camps, Sebago Wohelo, for girls 12–16, and Little Wohelo, for girls 6–12. Each is compact, yet thoughtfully laid out, with wonderful 1908-vintage buildings spread along the waterfront. Little Wohelo was probably the first camp in the country exclusively for younger children and continues to be entirely separate from Sebago Wohelo, the camps being located a mile apart.

Relations between the sister camps remain close, however. Little Wohelo girls are chosen as summer sisters by the Sebago Wohelo girls, and the two camps get together frequently for special events. Programs in both camps are similar, differing mainly in levels of challenge as well as in camper autonomy. For example, where Little Wohelo's program is basically structured (girls may choose some of their activities), a Sebago Wohelo camper chooses entirely how she will spend her time, from the kinds of activities she will take to whether or not she wants to take several different things or specialize in only one or two.

Because of the exceptional waterfront—Wohelo maintains a floating H-dock, four cribwork docks, twenty-seven sailboats, six rowboats, two waterski boats, two large inboard boats, Windsurfers, and over thirty canoes—swimming and boating are emphasized here. Other activities are those that are geared toward lifetime skills, such as tennis (the camp has six courts), choral singing, diving, sailing regattas, dancing, crafts, ecology and nature activities, animal care, campcraft, tripping, tumbling, dramatics, and a terrific arts and crafts program, with the best jewelry-making program I've seen.

The girls of Little Wohelo, in addition to the above, also enjoy archery, paddle-wheel boating, puppetry, games, and playground activities. There are frequent special events and cookouts at both camps, as well as get-togethers with the boys of brother camp Timanous, another fine camp started by the founders of Wohelo, Dr. and Mrs. Luther Halsey Gulick.

This camp is justifiably proud of its heritage, and that pride is reflected in an uncommon stability. Counselors are mostly Wohelo alumni, and most of them return to their camp every summer. The directors are third and fourth generation, with succeeding generations likely to follow. Campers themselves keep returning from a wide geographical area.

The reasons for Wohelo's success may be numerous, but one thing is clear. This is an institution that emphasizes the business of building friendships and learning about yourself so that you build esteem. These people create a relaxed environment close to nature—no radios, no electricity in cabins, etc.—so that the sometimes complicated task of growing up is not only simplified but also enriched with support, spirituality, and genuine caring.

Wyonegonic
Camps for Girls

Address:
RR 1, Box 186
Denmark, Maine 04022

Phone:
(207) 452-2051

Natural features:
300 acres of pine forest bordering 2½ miles of lakefront

Nearest large city or town:
Northwest of Sebago Lake

Enrollment:
Girls

Age spread:
8–18

Per summer:
250 (181 per session)

Campers come from the:
Northeast 65% Southeast 7% Central 5% Northwest 3% Southwest 5% International 15%

Average number of international campers:
40—Venezuela 12, Spain 8, Germany 6, France 4, Austria 2, Mexico 2, Russia 2

Season:
June 28–August 15

Session (by percentage of campers) and cost:
3½ weeks, 40%, $2,375
7 weeks, 60%, $3,975

Extra charges:
None

Scholarships:
10% of campers do not pay full tuition

Financial structure:
For profit

Founded:
1902—the oldest organized girls' camp in the United States; Wyonegonic and Winona are the country's oldest sister/brother camps

Owner(s) and years associated with camp:
Carol Sudduth, 35

Managing Director(s) and years associated with camp:
Carol Sudduth, 35

Director's background:
Carol Sudduth: B.S., education, University of Wisconsin; teacher; recreation leader

Counselors: 60
Men 15% Women 85% Min. age 19
Ratio to campers 1: 4

Health and safety:
Infirmary, 2 RNs on staff; hospital 10 minutes away

Concentration:
"Training of staff, supervising the well-being of campers, health and safety, quality of the program." Activities include canoeing and sailing, archery, riding, tennis, riflery, canoe/hiking trips, campcraft, and arts and crafts."

Mission:
"We are in the child development business. Four cornerstones of our philosophy are health, happiness, friendship and individual growth, all within the framework of an appreciation for the out-of-doors. We offer this in a non-competitive atmosphere with campers from over 30 states and foreign countries."

Wyonegonic and her brother camp, Winona, are practically carbon copies of one another; in other words, a better camp would be hard to find. For starters, Wyonegonic is the oldest girls' camp in the country, run by very experienced people and grounded in the very best traditions of American camping.

Since much of the twelve-mile Moose Pond belongs to the two camps (Wyonegonic alone has two and a half miles of lakefront), there is a strong feeling of privacy and isolation here, enhanced by the rustic beauty of Pleasant Mountain, which rises up from the western shore. Set among three hundred acres of pine forest, the camp's bark-faced buildings seem like part of the woods themselves.

Wyonegonic is actually three camps, with separate programs and facilities for each of its three age groups. There are forty Juniors, ages 8–11; sixty Intermediates, ages 11–13; and sixty Seniors, ages 13–16. The focus here is on the child. Camp activities are not seen as ends in themselves but as tools to promote self-confidence, an appreciation of the outdoors, and personal relationships. The emphasis is on cooperation, not competition. Therefore, activities such as hiking, sailing, canoeing, and tripping get more attention than, say, team sports.

Flexibility within a general structure is the keynote of all three camps. Each camper designs her own program from a wide range of possibilities, with activities geared so that she can progress gradually through higher levels of challenge and competence.

Water activities are the most popular; appropriately, the three waterfronts (for swimming, sailing, and canoeing) are of the highest quality. Swimming is taught by American Red Cross instructors and includes lifeguarding, water survival, and both long distance and synchronized swimming. Sailing instruction is offered on a new fleet of eight Vanguard 15s, which are rigged with a mainsail and a jib. Sailors may choose a racing program as their skills develop (every year Wyonegonic hosts a regatta to which seven other girls' and boys' camps are invited). There are also two smaller boats and four sailboards that may be used for recreation, as well as a fleet of forty-four canoes that are used on the lake and on many of Maine's rivers. Water-skiing is also available to Senior campers.

Land activities include tennis (on six clay tennis courts), archery, and riflery. English-style horseback riding teaches girls how to care for a mount and participate in horse shows. A stable and training ring with jumps augment many miles of trails on Wyonegonic property. Other popular activities include pottery and other crafts, dance, gymnastics, aerobics, and music.

Each day, time is set aside for a girl to be alone, to read a book or write letters or simply sit somewhere and relax. Twice a week all three camps get together for special occasions, such as Banquet Night or Candlenight. And on Sunday after-noons the "brothers" from Winona come to visit from up the lake.

Trips, which typically include a trip leader, assistant, and eight campers, range from one to five days and extend from paddling down the gentle Saco River to white-water canoeing on the Allagash; and from climbing nearby Pleasant Moun-tain to backpacking on Mount Katahdin and the White Mountains.

Even in its dining, Wyonegonic succeeds in maintaining a small-camp feeling. The dining room is attractive, woodsy, and traditional, with plaques hanging over fireplaces. Meals are intimate, and the food is always good.

The camp's large international population is well served by Wyonegonic's pro-nounced interest in international peace and sisterhood. Displayed in the rec hall are forty-eight flags representing the home countries of recent campers. There's a real family feeling here, a place of warmth and security, caring, and lots of support. No matter where on this campus you happen to wander, or when you're there, you never get the sense that this is anything but a splendid place for a growing girl to spend a few summer weeks.

About the Authors

Richard C. Kennedy was director of Camp Kieve in Nobleboro, Maine, where he still lives. He had worked with children—as a teacher, camp counselor, and camp director—for more than thirty-five years.

Michael Kimball is the author of a novel, *Firewater Pond,* as well as several television shows and magazine articles. He has worked as a schoolteacher and as director of a summer education program for the children of migrant workers. He lives in Coopers Mills, Maine.